WITHDRAWN FROM
TCC LIBRARY
TALLAHASSEE
COMMUNITY COLLEGE
LIBRARY

D1378460

20TH-CENTURY COMPOSERS

Hindemith, Hartmann and Henze

Hindemith, Hartmann and Henze

by Guy Rickards

For Alison, Katherine and Jennifer

Phaidon Press Limited
Regent's Wharf
All Saints Street
London N1 9PA

First published 1995

ISBN 0 7148 3174 3

A CIP catalogue record for this book is available from the British Library

Printed in Singapore

Frontispiece, Paul Hindemith, composer and conductor of international renown, in characteristic pose on the rostrum, late 1950s

Contents

Preface

In writing this intertwined biography of three composers I have inevitably drawn on the experience and assistance of many individuals, which accumulation of debt I must now happily and gratefully acknowledge. The wide disparity of published source materials available for each of the three men can be seen in the bibliography. I have been fortunate to have had access to the personal recollections – many not previously published – of those individuals who knew Hindemith, Hartmann or Henze or who had experience of life in Germany at crucial periods. On the negative side, the response from several eminent figures was disappointing; I encountered a certain amount of resistance from some, especially concerning the period of the Nazi tyranny and the person of Karl Amadeus Hartmann. Perhaps the past proved too painful to recall. One who had no such qualms is the sole surviving subject of this book, Hans Werner Henze. I am deeply in his debt for taking time out from his crowded schedule to talk to me at length about his life and work, and his dealings with Hartmann, for whom he has retained a great devotion. I have quoted liberally from my interview with him and his subsequent letters. And I must record here my thanks to Faber and Faber Ltd for granting permission to quote from Peter Labanyi's translation for Henze's autobiographical writings – *Music and Politics.* Others who gave freely of their memories, and whose correspondence proved most enlightening, were Danish composer, Vagn Holmboe and his wife, Meta Graf; Mme Madeleine Milhaud; Icelandic composer, Jon Thórarinsson; Dr Giselher Schubert of the Paul Hindemith Institute in Frankfurt am Main; Andras Briner; Finnish composer, Paavo Heininen; Lotte Klemperer, daughter of the renowned conductor, Otto Klemperer; British composers, Robert Simpson and John McCabe; conductor, Gary Brain; and most especially, Frau Elisabeth Hartmann, widow of Karl Amadeus.

Others who helped in more general ways with information, scores, recordings and so forth were Dr Andrew D. McCredie, the sole previous biographer of Hartmann; Martin Anderson of Toccata Press; James Jolly and Harriet Smith of *Gramophone*; Michael Stewart; composer and author, Malcolm Macdonald; Siegmund Nissel, formerly of the Amadeus String Quartet; composer, Berthold Goldschmidt; Dr Tomi Mäkelä; Margaret Truscott, widow of the distinguished writer on music and composer, Harold Truscott; Erik Levi; Nuria Schoenberg-Nono; Andreas K. W. Meyer of the German record company Classic Produktion Osnabrück; Karen Pitchford at Koch International Ltd; Anne-Louise Hyde Crofts at Conifer Records Ltd; the staff at Harmonia Mundi (UK) Ltd; David Denton; Scott Butler; David J. Harris of Spargo Consulting; Dr Alan Marshall; and the staff of Schott Music International, the publishers for all three composers: in London, Sally Groves and Ulrike Müller; in Mainz, Katja Engelhardt, Almuth Willing, and most particularly Klaus Rainer Schöll, who was unstinting in his efforts on my behalf and who acted as a go-between for me with Frau Hartmann.

Rupert Gates I must thank, especially for his quick and elegant translations of Hartmann's autobiographical writings; the series editor, Norman Lebrecht, for allowing me the scope to tackle the book in my own way; the staff at Phaidon for their not inconsiderable work in making the book look as good as it does; and lastly, but not least, my wife and children who had to put up with me being for so long in another time and place.

Guy Rickards
Horsham, 1995

The German Question

The German Question – what the medieval world might quaintly have termed the Matter of Germany – has been one of the central concerns of European history of the past thousand years, and almost no area of modern life or activity is without its own often controversial variant on it. In its most basic terms, the Question might simply be expressed 'What of Germany?' or 'What to do about Germany?'. Twice in the first half of the twentieth century the Question's political ramifications engulfed the planet in global conflict of a previously unimaginable scale and horror. After 1945, the divided Germany became the central catalyst of the Cold War and, in the breaching of the Berlin Wall in 1990, has provided perhaps the single most celebrated event of recent world history. The shock waves of the Wall's moral and physical demolition are still reverberating through the public consciousness and, even if other events have come to dominate the foreground, the Matter of Germany is squarely back on the agenda of world affairs. In purely musical terms, the Question is concerned with what happened in Germany contemporary with these events, how its dominant position in Western music was destroyed and to what extent it has recovered since.

Culturally, Germany has occupied a primary position in Western civilization over the past four centuries, an important element of which has been the legacy of her composers. The bedrock of Western music's instrumental, chamber and orchestral concert repertory is provided by German composers – even if one does not count those from Austria as German – especially those of the eighteenth and nineteenth centuries. In the theatre, German opera, alongside that from Italy, provides the cornerstone of the established repertoire. In the present century, when politics and music have collided as never before, it was in Germany that composers first found themselves under fire for non-musical reasons and their work has acquired an extraneous significance that is unparalleled outside of Soviet Russia.

This book is not intended as a political history of Germany in the present century, nor is it an examination of the intrusiveness of the political into musical life, although inevitably aspects of these concerns must colour the narrative. The aim here is to provide a linked biography, set in the wider historical context, of the three German composers who collectively have been central to the development of the core tradition of German music inherited from the previous century: Paul Hindemith (1895–1963), Karl Amadeus Hartmann (1905–63) and Hans Werner Henze (b. 1926). Despite markedly different approaches and political sensibilities, all three in turn nurtured and extended this tradition by uniting the spirit of experiment with orthodox German expression.

German music in the latter half of the nineteenth century had been divided into two camps, each centred on a particular figurehead composer. One, surrounding Johannes Brahms, extolled a classical viewpoint with Brahms as the direct and natural heir of the Viennese Classical masters – Joseph Haydn, Wolfgang Amadeus Mozart and Ludwig van Beethoven. The opposed camp were Romantics by orientation and grouped about the outsize persona of Richard Wagner, whose music had probably pushed back the boundaries of music further than anyone. The composers of the Classical Period, extending roughly from the death of Johann Sebastian Bach in 1750, to that of Beethoven in 1827, had maintained a common language in composition that took little account of ethnic and political boundaries. But the rise of the Romantic Movement in art and literature inevitably caught music in its wake and engendered the development of a more personal voice in composition. Common traits of Romantic music at its height across the continent were the inclusion of overtly nationalist elements, often folk-dances and folk-songs, and a propensity for works illustrating a non-musical programme, as in the *Symphonie fantastique* of the Frenchman, Hector Berlioz, and the Symphonic Poems of the Hungarian, Franz Liszt. Occasionally, these elements would combine in depicting subjects from history or mythology, as with the opera *Boris Godunov* by Modest Mussorgsky or Wagner's tetralogy of music-dramas, *Der Ring des Nibelungen.*

The division between classicizing and romantic forces continued in German music into the twentieth century. The character of the music associated with each group, however, began to change and the distinctions between them to blur. Crossover figures emerged, of whom the most prophetic and important was the German–Italian, Ferruccio Busoni (1866–1924). Busoni promulgated new ideas designed to unify the polarities in German music in a doctrine of 'youthful classicality'. This was sternly resisted by conservative figures such as Hans Pfitzner (1869–1949). In fact, many composers alternated between the two ideals at different times in their careers, as Brahms and Wagner had done. Broadly speaking, the music of Gustav Mahler (1860–1911) came to epitomize the continued Romantic tradition of music. This was highlighted by his famous remark to the Finnish composer, Jean Sibelius (1865–1957), that the symphony, his preferred form, 'must be like the world – it must be all-embracing'.

The music of Max Reger (1873–1916), by contrast, breathed new life into the Classical forms of earlier centuries. The dominant figure of the first twenty years of the twentieth century, however, was undoubtedly the Bavarian, Richard Strauss (1864–1949). He had been a friend and rival of Mahler's, and his operas and symphonic poems enjoyed – and many still do – a success unrivalled since Wagner's day. He was unashamedly romantic in spirit, although in his last few years composed music of a lucid quality that was anything but romantic in outlook.

In the first decade of the twentieth century a new type of music arose which polarized composers and their audiences more than ever before. Atonality was a logical development from certain trends within the Romantic camp and principally affected the harmonic properties of the music that used it. Music written in an atonal style undermined, and in more progressive hands rejected outright, the traditional tonal basis of European music, with its hierarchical structure of notes rooted on the key (first) and dominant (fifth) notes of the major/minor scales. Atonal music tended to treat the twelve notes of the chromatic scale equally, without assigning particular significance to any one. (On a piano this difference can be heard by comparing the scale of C major – all the white notes, with the chromatic scale – the white and black notes played in ascending sequence.) Just as Romanticism had been inspired by a literary and artistic movement in the nineteenth century, so atonality became associated with Expressionism, a lurid development of Romanticism in the early years of this century before the Great War, again rooted in literature and painting. The new music shocked and scandalized audiences, often causing disturbances and protests in concert halls during performances. The driving force behind the spread of atonality was Arnold Schoenberg (1874–1951), of mixed Hungarian, Austrian and Czech origins. He collected around him in Vienna a like-minded group or school of composers who shared a devotion to the music of Mahler and a willingness to explore the uncharted territory Schoenberg had opened up. The most prominent members of this group were the apprentice Austrian composers Alban Berg (1885–1935) and Anton von Webern (1883–1945). One of the special features of the works of Schoenberg and his colleagues was the synthesis of many of the disparate stylistic features of the music of Brahms and Wagner, a process that Mahler had begun. The Second Viennese School laid the foundations upon which German music after 1945 was built.

Between them, Schoenberg and Webern were to remould atonal composition on a rigorous intellectual basis, imposing upon its free evolution of harmony and melody a classical severity of application. This and other developments in German music had far-reaching consequences for the future direction of music in Europe and the Americas as a whole. Not that outside influences were ignored: innovative techniques found in the works of foreign masters such as the Russian, Igor Stravinsky (1882–1971), and Hungarian, Béla Bartók (1881–1945) were absorbed as fluently as home-grown ideas. German musicians and composers were at the forefront of new music during the years of the Weimar Republic (1920–33) between the two World Wars and in the Federal Republic after 1945. Hindemith in particular was associated with this pioneering spirit during the 1920s, as was Henze in the late 1940s and 1950s. In between these periods of rampant experimentation occurred a nightmare of oppression when all such adventure was stopped dead in its tracks by the political ideologues of the Nazi party. Germany between 1933 and 1945 was denuded of most of its wealth of artistic and scientific talent by the racist policies of the Third Reich. Almost all progressive artistic work was banned, the Nazis attempting forcibly to erase the internationalist trends embodied in the new music festivals by cultivating a boorishly nationalist idiom. After the collapse of the Third Reich in 1945, a violent backlash against this dislocation of musical development was inevitable. An essential part of the post-war revivification of German musical culture was the aggressively radical movement, led by Karlheinz Stockhausen and his French colleague, Pierre Boulez, centred on the annual composers' summer school at Darmstadt.

Hindemith, although an undoubted radical in the early 1920s, opted, by the end of that decade, to follow a more conservative and personal path. While continuing to promote new compositions by his contemporaries up until the early 1930s, he turned his back on active experimentation himself. Indeed in the introductory chapter to the first volume of his book *Unterweisung im Tonsatz* ('The Craft of Musical Composition'), he wrote:

> *It is not surprising that things have developed as they have. The discovery, in the last century, of the extreme limits of power and subtlety in the effect of the musical tone extended the boundaries of the tonal domain at the disposal of the composer into hitherto undreamed-of distances. New combinations of tones came to be recognized, and new ways of bending a melodic line were discovered. It seemed as if the sun had risen upon a new, glowing, iridescent land, into which our musician–discoverers rushed headlong. Blinded by the immense store of materials never used before, deafened by the fantastic novelty of sound, everyone seized without reflection on whatever he felt he could use. At this point instruction failed. Either it fell into the same frenzy as practice, and devoted itself to flimsy speculation, instead of adapting its systems of teaching to the new material, or it lapsed into inactivity, and what had never been a very strong urge towards novelty turned into a barren clinging to the past. Confidence in inherited methods vanished; they seemed barely adequate now to guide the beginner's first steps. Whoever wished to make any progress gave himself unreservedly to the New, neither helped nor hindered by theoretical instruction, which had simply become inadequate to the occasion.*

This was a situation that would be repeated again after 1945. It is deeply ironic that in this passage Hindemith gave expression, arising from purely musical considerations, to a reasoned rejection of much of the music that was banned and classed as degenerate by the Nazis.

Although his own music (and his book) suffered a similar fate Hindemith was, in certain areas, in accord with the thinking of the Nazi cultural administration, though not of course with their thuggish methods.

Taken together, Hindemith, Hartmann and Henze never formed a coherent school of composition or even a like-minded group such as the Russian 'Mighty Handful' or France's *Les Six*. They came from different backgrounds, geographical locations and generations. Whilst they all knew of and individually met each other, it would seem that they never all came together at one time and in one place. Yet their lives and work were indissolubly interconnected, as much because of the turmoil of two World Wars and the ensuing political chaos as for any purely aesthetic reasons. As will be seen, there are some remarkable parallels between their careers, particularly during the crucial period when the Nazis were in power and in the aftermath of the German defeat, though the net stretches rather wider than the twelve catastrophic years of the Third Reich. For example, Hindemith's and Hartmann's forebears both came, at one or two removes, from Silesia on the eastern marches of pre-Great War Germany, although they themselves were brought up in the west of the country. Hindemith's and Henze's fathers both volunteered for active military service in their mid-forties, in 1914 and 1944 respectively, and both were killed, during conflicts in which their budding composer sons also served. Most tellingly, perhaps, all three suffered exile or alienation from German life. Hindemith did so on personal as much as musical grounds after 1937 – and not for ideological or racial reasons. Hartmann had already withdrawn into 'internal emigration' by that time, remaining in Germany but refusing to have any truck with the Nazis or their musical establishment. After the war, Henze became disgusted at the state of the emergent Federal republic in the west of the newly divided Germany and its heavy reliance on the old Fascist governmental and social apparatus, factors which helped to make his continued residence in his homeland untenable. Yet, as I hope this study will affirm, one of the most fascinating aspects of their parallel lives is their wholly divergent reactions to similar external events and pressures.

I

Prelude 1895–1914

Paul Hindemith aged eighteen, on the eve of the First World War

He was not born for the classics, nor does he fit the role of the 'old master'. To me, he will always remain the fresh gay musician that he is.

Otto Klemperer on Hindemith,
Minor Recollections, 1964

Prelude 1895–1914

The Germany into which Paul Hindemith was born, in Hanau near Frankfurt am Main, on 16 November 1895 was one of industry, optimism and burgeoning power. Since its creation, following the Prussian victory on the fields of Sadowa and Sedan between 1866 and 1871, the Second Reich had transformed the loose confederation of petty German states into a rapidly expanding world power, with huge African colonial territories and interests stretching from South America to the Chinese coast. At home, a succession of relatively liberal chancellors was slowly dispelling the domestic tensions of the troubled final years of Bismarck's tenure of office.

Paul Hindemith was of humble origins, unlike most composers at this time who were drawn from the middle and upper echelons of society. His mother's family were of peasant stock. She was born Marie Sophie Warnecke in the small Hessian town of Stammen, on 29 January 1868. She married his father, Robert Rudolph Emil Hindemith, her junior by two years, on 23 March 1895. Robert Hindemith came from the opposite side of Germany, born in the little Silesian town of Naumburg, near Breslau (modern-day Wrocław in Poland), on 15 May 1870, the son of a Protestant artisan father by his Catholic third wife. The coexistence of Lutheran and Roman ideology under one roof seems to have been an uneasy one which proved to be a continuing source of friction and accounts for Paul Hindemith's undogmatic attitude to religion.

Robert Hindemith had been forced by economic pressures to move west in order to improve his prospects. Stern and hard-working, he possessed no particular talents, other than a propensity to play the zither, and succeeded only in eking out a precarious and fitful living through a succession of manual and menial jobs. His principal achievement as a father was to foster a hearty detestation of himself in his children, particularly his sons. To his credit, he did recognize that they had inherited a natural talent, but in driving his children's musicality hard from an early age, he could have killed their love of music stone dead. There is no evidence that, as Hindemith's pupil Walter Leigh claimed in 1936, 'Hindemith ran away from home in order to pursue a musical career.' Parental approval was not in any doubt. Robert would take his offspring to the local opera, often on foot. After performances the children would be tested long and rigorously to see how much they had learned, earning smacks if their response failed to please. At other times Robert put them on show in a quartet with himself playing zither, his son Paul and daughter Toni

The Hindemith family, photographed c. 1899 (left to right): Paul, father Robert, baby Toni, mother Marie; younger brother Rudolf was born the following year.

violins, and younger son Rudolf the cello. Despite this crude and exploitative upbringing, Paul and Rudolf went on to make successful careers as performers, Rudolf becoming the cellist in the Amar String Quartet (in which Paul played the viola) as well as playing in the State Opera in Vienna.

For the first few years of Paul's life, the Hindemith family led a nomadic existence in and around the Frankfurt area as Robert sought sustained employment to support his growing family. Paul spent some time with his grandparents in Silesia. Resources were stretched desperately thin when Robert was out of work. Friends attempted to give the family some money for the children to carry on with their musical studies, but Robert and Marie refused.

Financial strictures, however severe, did not prevent the eight-year-old Paul from being sent for violin lessons, first with a local teacher in Mühlheim; later, aged ten, to Anna Hegner, a Swiss violinist who led her own string quartet. In 1908, still not thirteen, he was sent to Adolf Rebner, a deeply musical, if conservative and academic-minded, Austrian teacher at the Hoch Conservatory in Frankfurt. Rebner knew talent when he heard it. He admitted Paul to the Conservatory and later installed him as second violinist in his own quartet. (After the First World War Hindemith switched to the viola.)

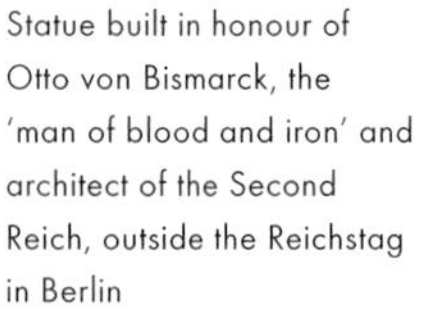
Statue built in honour of Otto von Bismarck, the 'man of blood and iron' and architect of the Second Reich, outside the Reichstag in Berlin

Above left, Hindemith, with his violin tutor Anna Hegner in 1907
Above, the student Hindemith aged fourteen, in 1910

Colonial expansion: Kaiser Wilhelm II, Emperor of Germany (seated on a white charger in the centre of the picture) at the head of German troops parading through Tangiers in 1905

An official photographic portrait of Kaiser Wilhelm II taken in 1902

The Hoch Conservatory was founded in 1878 under Liszt's associate, Joseph Joachim Raff, and numbered on its faculty Schumann's widow, Clara, and Engelbert Humperdinck, composer of *Hänsel und Gretel*. Hindemith arrived just as Iwan Knorr took over as director, ushering in a period of regeneration and the establishment of a school orchestra. Knorr was widely respected as a pedagogue, whose pupils included the composers Cyril Scott, Hans Pfitzner (who caused a scandal in 1899 by eloping with the daughter of his piano tutor) and Ernst Toch. After the harsh impecunious climate at home, this sudden move into a more exalted atmosphere was exactly what the young Hindemith needed.

Robert Hindemith could not afford to pay fees for both sons, Rudolf having enrolled in the cello class in 1910. Both boys attended on a free scholarship at Rebner's recommendation. Paul's initial progress was sufficiently good for him to start making regular solo appearances at end-of-term Conservatory concerts from 1909, at first in straightforward Baroque fare, later graduating, in 1911, to Mozart's Violin Concerto in D major, K 218 (albeit the first movement only) and Bach's great Chaconne from the Solo Partita in D minor, BWV 1004. Paul and Rudolf also played together in string and piano quartets, inside and outside the Conservatory, thereby augmenting the family income.

There were no financial pressures in the early life of Karl Amadeus Hartmann, born on 2 August 1905, in the Catholic State of Bavaria, the youngest of four brothers who would all outlive him. Hartmann's father, Friedrich Richard, had been born in 1866, the year of the Battle of Sadowa, his mother, Gertrud (née Schwamm), eight years later, both to families of Silesian origin. Hartmann's family had strong artistic and artisan traditions: his paternal grandfather, also named Friedrich, had established himself in Muhnau in Silesia as a cabinet-maker of local distinction and Hartmann's father had built a successful career in Munich as a schoolteacher and a painter specializing in flowers. Hartmann defined his father – known by his middle name, Richard – as 'a person who was wrapped up in his own world of ideas and possessed of a wanderlust. This took him above all to France and Italy, where he spent many years. Whenever one accompanied him to an exhibition he looked absorbed and hardly ever judged anything. He always encouraged young people to look about them and observe contemporary trends in art.' Of his mother, Hartmann wrote that she 'had a great gift for music' and possessed 'a powerfully expressive character', having 'a living relationship with music – especially songs and opera. Wagner was her idol. She read Balzac and Zola with

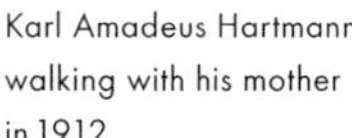

Karl Amadeus Hartmann walking with his mother in 1912

Bernhard Sekles, composer and Hindemith's composition teacher at the Hoch Conservatory from 1913

particular affection. She could sit and tell us children stories for hours on end.' Of those children the eldest, Adolf, later became a distinguished portrait painter.

The family lived in settled, harmonious, though frugal circumstances. 'Karl never got new shoes, he had to wear the old shoes of his elder brothers,' his widow recalls. Richard and Gertrud Hartmann none the less fostered the varied artistic ambitions of their sons. Not infrequently the whole family – and any guests to hand – would be involved in impromptu theatrical performances at home. Politically, the family tended towards Democratic Socialism, left-wing in orientation but liberal and independent in spirit. Adolf in particular followed his parents' political persuasions and exercised a lasting influence on his youngest brother, Karl. This dissidence was hardened by the national trauma of World War I.

It was in the years leading up to the outbreak of war in 1914 that the young Hindemith began to compose clandestinely – mainly to avoid the unwelcome scrutiny of his teachers and peers – often ruling out his own music stave paper to avoid expense. Several pieces were written for cello, including five sonatas, three of them unaccompanied, obviously with his brother in mind, as well as two piano trios, a string quartet and around twenty songs. Very few of these early compositions survived the partial destruction of the family home during Second World War air-raids. In 1912 Arnold Mendelssohn,

Following page, a factory of the Allgemeine Elektricitäts-Gesellschaft (AEG) in Berlin, one of the many companies which contributed to the German industrial might during the 1900s

ALLGEMEINE ELEKTRICITÄTS-GE
Halt!
Halt!

Tragkraft 20 Tonnen.

second cousin of the celebrated composer Felix Mendelssohn, arrived at the Conservatory as professor of composition. At the following end-of-year concert in 1913, Hindemith made his début as a composer when a fellow student performed a short set of Variations in E flat minor on an unknown theme for the piano – also lost. Sometime between 1913 and 1915, he began to write a series of short plays, some in verse, others in prose, of adolescent biographical and allegorical nature. A common thread of these plays is the constriction of an individual's freedom by stultifying demands to practise a musical instrument. In one, *Viola Mania*, the hero attempts to kill his boss through an 'ordeal-by-viola', in response to the latter's incessant demands. He fails and duly commits suicide in the bathroom.

Hindemith's compositional freedom was short-lived; after the summer break of 1913, Bernhard Sekles, Frankfurt-born and a former Hoch pupil, took over from Mendelssohn and imposed a stricter, more rigorous and authoritarian regime on the composition class. Hindemith may have chafed at the bit, but the thorough grounding he received in the technical craft of creating a piece of music was to be of immeasurable benefit. Sekles, for all the discipline that he enforced, was not unprogressive in outlook. In 1925 he would organize a seminar on jazz in collaboration with the young Hungarian composer Mátyás Seiber. However, at this crucial juncture in Hindemith's education, the cosy, secluded world of the Conservatory was abruptly and irreversibly shattered. On 28 June 1914, Archduke Ferdinand, heir to the Habsburg throne of the Austrian Empire, was assassinated with his wife in Sarajevo, and the continent of Europe plunged into war.

2

War and Revolution 1914–20

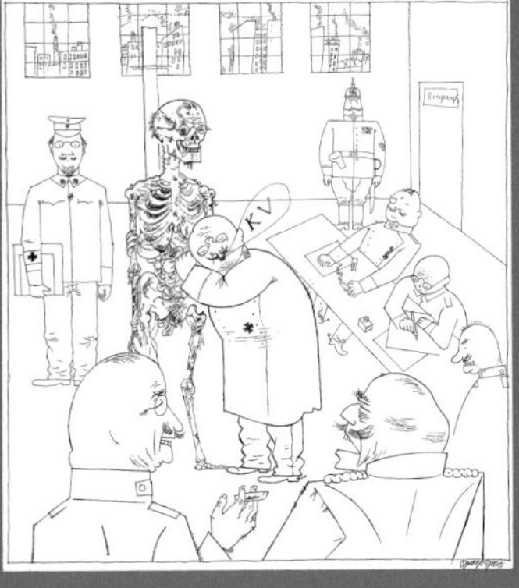

'Fit for Active Service': a First World War cartoon by George Grosz satirizing the German High Command's desperate search for manpower

... War with Germany, it is a terrible catastrophe but it is not our fault. An enormous crowd collected outside the Palace; we went on the balcony both before and after dinner. When they heard that War had been declared, the excitement increased and May and I with David went onto the balcony; the cheering was terrific.

King George V of Great Britain,
diary entry for 4 August 1914

War and Revolution 1914–20

By August 1914, the tangle of alliance and counter-alliance designed to maintain a balance of power in Europe had created a situation of the utmost fragility whereby the death of one man could force the major powers into battle. Thus, Austria declared war on Serbia, the country held responsible for the Archduke's death, and Russia mobilized her armies in the latter's support. This obliged Germany to stand with Austria and France to join Russia. Britain was sucked in by treaty commitments to France and Belgium. When hostilities commenced, there was a widespread popular enthusiasm for war, especially in Germany where, the previous year, General Bernhardi had scored a notable literary success with his bloodthirsty treatise, *Vom heutigen Kriege* ('Of Today's War'), extolling the virtue of battle as a necessary process for civilization to rid itself of its bad blood. The euphoria was

Extra-Blatt

Berliner Lokal-Anzeiger

Sonnabend, 1. August. 1914.

Allgemeine Mobilmachung in Deutschland.

Die zwölfstündige Frist, die Deutschland der russischen Regierung zur Abgabe einer loyalen Erklärung gestellt hat, ist ergebnislos verstrichen. Soeben ist der Befehl des Kaisers ergangen, der die sofortige Mobilmachung der gesamten deutschen Streitkräfte anordnet.

Alle Extra-Ausgaben des Berliner Lokal-Anzeigers werden nach wie vor in beliebiger Anzahl gratis in unseren sämtlichen Expeditionen an jedermann ausgegeben.

An Imperial conscription notice of August 1914, announcing 'General Mobilization in Germany'

Ready for the fray: German troops en route to France, August 1914

not restricted to Germany, however; millions of men across Europe volunteered to fight in a war that nearly everyone believed 'would be over by Christmas'.

Late in the war Paul wrote to Emmy Ronnefeldt: 'It's as well that I am not religious or I'd have long since done battle with God. These cursed people who keep the war going should come here [to the front] for a holiday – they would learn quickly.'

So unexpected was the onset of war that Hindemith had been out of the country at the time, playing the violin in a small band as a summer job in a holiday resort in Switzerland. Robert Hindemith, aged forty-four, volunteered for military service. He received orders to go to France at the end of June 1915, and Paul had to shoulder the burden of responsibility as bread-winner. He gave up his scholarship at Hoch, but continued to attend Sekles' composition classes for another two years until being called up himself. On 24 June he joined the Frankfurt Opera orchestra at a salary of 1,200 marks per annum which left him slightly better paid than the majority of manual and white-collar workers. Within three months he was appointed *Konzertmeister*, leading the first violins and occasionally acting as a soloist in concertos. Away from the opera pit, the orchestra was usually conducted by Willem Mengelberg, chief conductor of the Concertgebouw Orchestra in Amsterdam. Mengelberg had a considerable international reputation but Hindemith was unimpressed with him personally and musically, as some early letters of his reveal.

Following page, with their menfolk at the Front, German women took their places in the munitions factories and other industries, to help the war economy.

Frankfurt Opera House, c. 1920, where Hindemith was *Konzertmeister* from 1915–22

'My enemy' he calls him, 'a nasty, inconsiderate person ... how passionately I loathe him.' He found the music under Mengelberg's direction often 'mauled', 'unmusical' or 'brutal'.

He also played second violin in Rebner's string quartet and began taking private students for violin instruction. His enforced maturity was accelerated by his father's death in Belgium on 25 September 1915, though the news did not reach the Hindemith family until the following spring.

Hindemith's promotion to *Konzertmeister* brought him closer to the musical director of Frankfurt Opera, Ludwig Rottenberg, whose daughter he married nine years later. He also came within the orbit of other affluent families, not least the Ronnefeldts, whose daughter Emmy studied piano at the Hoch. Paul's letters to Emmy are full of personal revelations and opinions, although after his return from active service, they appear to have drifted apart. By contrast, he established a lasting rapport musically with Emma Lübbecke-Job, who gave many premières of his piano works through the 1920s.

As a composer, Hindemith produced his first three officially listed works during these first eighteen months of the war: an *Andante and Scherzo* for clarinet, horn and piano, a String Quartet in C major which won the Mendelssohn Prize (a much-needed windfall), and his first orchestral piece, the Cello Concerto in E flat major. Composed in 1915, the concerto is barely recognizable as being by Hindemith at all. Its opening flourish is suggestive of the music of Richard Strauss, while later on there are stylistic debts to Brahms and Antonín Dvořák. The première – probably Hindemith's public début as a conductor – was given at a Hoch Conservatory concert on 28 June 1916 with his friend Maurits Frank as soloist. Of his three concertos for the cello, this first, only rediscovered in the 1970s, has been overshadowed by the later *Kammermusik* No. 3 (1925) and the Cello Concerto of 1940.

A measure of Hindemith's growing confidence can be gauged from his very next work, the *Lustige Sinfonietta*. The literal translation would be 'Merry Little Symphony', although *Lustige* carries the connotation of 'vivacious' or 'full of life', not unlike the archaic English 'lusty'. Composed between February and August 1916, it was inspired by the poetry of Christian Morgenstern; in the only recording of the work the verses are declaimed unaccompanied, the music acting as much as a foil to the texts as a displaced setting of them. The eight numbers reveal the full impact of Richard Strauss's music on the developing composer; they form a chain, grouped into three movements only outwardly resembling a symphonic plan. Whilst the *Lustige Sinfonietta* is a light-hearted, at times parodical affair, it is not entirely so; for all its irreverence, it is the first work in which a personal tone became manifest and the final few numbers are possessed of a symphonic thrust and grasp of pace that betokened well for the future. Alas, no one but Hindemith could have known this, the work not being performed until 1980.

The pianist Emma Lübbecke-Job, a long-standing friend and champion of Hindemith's music, c. 1920

What future that might be was becoming increasingly uncertain as the war dragged on. Disillusion with the military situation in the wake of the failure of both the German 'Verdun' and British 'Somme' offensives was reinforced by the mounting death-toll, inducing governments to conscript replacements for their rapidly depleting armies and enforcing rationing and Draconian social policies to retain order. The severe famine in Germany during the 'turnip' winter of 1916–17, occasioned by the destruction of the potato crop due to early frosts, caused privation and hardship that the populace were ill-equipped to deal with; the reduction in the bread ration the following April prompted strikes and open protest up and down the country. Internally, Germany began to collapse: a naval mutiny broke out during the summer in Kiel; there were revolts in the Reichstag, unrest in the cities. Ignominious defeat faced her allies Austria–Hungary and Turkey, while unrestricted submarine warfare had damaged German prestige; its resumption in February 1917 was a key element in American's decision to enter the war.

The year 1917 was a good one for Hindemith's music: Breitkopf and Härtel accepted a set of Three Movements for Cello and Piano, Op. 8 – his first printed composition – and there were several new works including Three Songs for Voice and Orchestra, Op. 9. Additionally, Frankfurt Opera renewed his contract for four years at an increased salary. A few weeks later, he was conscripted, posted to the local barracks and, in the following January, transferred to France.

Hindemith's experience of active service seems unreal in the context of the appalling slaughter in Flanders. He was never required to serve in the trenches and rarely went near the front. Appointed to his regiment's military band as a drummer, he spent much of his time playing string quartets to his two successive colonels. In March 1918, during a recital of the Debussy Quartet, news reached them of the

General Hindenburg reviews marines on parade in Kiel, where mutinies were to break out in the last days of the war

Die Pleite

30 Pf. 1. Jahrgang, Nr. 3 Der Malik-Verlag, Berlin-Leipzig Anfang April 1919 30 Pf.

Prost Noske! — — das Proletariat ist entwaffnet!

'Cheers, Noske! The Proletariat is disarmed': a 1919 cartoon by George Grosz on the front cover of *Die Pleite*, caricaturing the German Defence Minister, Gustav Noske

French composer's death, an event which made as great an impact on all present as Hindenburg and Ludendorff's four-day-old 'Victory' offensive. With time to spare and an ensemble to hand, Hindemith composed a song cycle with string quartet accompaniment, *Melancholie*, to words by Morgenstern again; his official First Quartet in F minor, Op. 10; marches, songs and a Sonata in G minor for Solo Violin published eventually as Op.11 No. 6. The Quartet No. 1, for all its stylistic archaism, is music of technical fluency and accomplishment. He dedicated it to Emmy Ronnefeldt's parents.

The death of his first colonel, Graf von Keilmannsegg, and the losses inflicted on 8 August 1918, the 'Black Day of the German Army', disrupted Hindemith's equilibrium. Promoted to corporal, he was kept well away from the battle zone and shortly afterwards completed part of a new Sonata for Violin and Piano, Op. 11 No. 1, conceiving the idea for a series of instrumental sonatas whose execution was still twenty years in the future.

The face of war from which Hindemith's musical activities largely protected him: Romanian troops attack near Braila on the Eastern Front, during the Autumn Campaign of 1916

The birth-pangs of the Weimar Republic, 1918–20: *above*, Communists seize the Residenz in Munich, May 1919; *right*, 'The Founding of the German Republic': an official proclamation, November 1918

The Germany he returned to after demobilization in the first weeks of 1919 was in the throes of revolution. Naval mutinies had broken out at Wilhelmshaven and Kiel; the Kaiser had been coerced into abdication after a General Strike; General Ludendorff had fled for his life in disguise to Sweden; and a Socialist-led coalition led by Chancellor Ebert held tenuous power. The whole infrastructure of Germany was being overturned: the Second Reich had been swept away leaving a huge vacuum in which no single authority exercised control. Soldiers' and workers' councils, influenced by the soviet model of 1917, assumed local control and a national Constituent Assembly was convened in Weimar (chosen for its historic and cultural associations as well as its relative neutrality), on 6 January 1919. The birth-pangs of this Weimar Republic were protracted and terrible. In Berlin, in the first month of its existence, the newly formed Communist party attempted to seize power but was brutally put down, its leaders murdered. Further south, in the Social and Democratic Republic of Bavaria, civil unrest resulted in the assassination of the State President. Street fighting spread to most German cities: in Berlin in March 1919 over one thousand were killed, while in Munich a soviet-style commune was established in the Bavarian capital in early April by a coalition of Independents and Socialists. This too was suppressed at the end of that month with summary executions of left-wingers, leaving Bavaria ominously right-wing in orientation. Further unrest followed when the humiliating terms of the Treaty of Versailles were made public, particularly the wholesale surrender of territory to Belgium, Denmark, France and Poland and the loss of all the colonies.

Karl Amadeus Hartmann was only thirteen when the armistice was signed, and during the war his aesthetic education had continued unbroken. In 1915, at the age of ten, he encountered Weber's opera *Der Freischütz* at the Munich Court Opera, an experience which was to prove formative. The music of the 'Wolf's Glen' scene 'enchanted me and stimulated me to my first efforts at composing'. He encountered Schubert's 'Unfinished' Symphony in B minor and 'fell in love with the passionate melodic melancholy and the harmonic poetry which was ahead of its time by a long way'. The two-movement structure of the 'Unfinished' served as a model for the mature Hartmann's Third, Sixth and Eighth Symphonies. He also

Karl Amadeus Hartmann, photographed in 1917

heard the music of Robert Schumann, Gustav Mahler (who had died only a few years before, in 1911) and Richard Strauss, who assumed an increasingly dominant position in Hartmann's musical pantheon through the 1920s.

Despite the known left-wing sympathies of Hartmann's father and eldest brother, the family as a whole does not seem to have been drawn into the turbulence of the post-war communes. Nor did they suffer in the ensuing purges, but these events and the family's political isolation left their mark. In September 1919, Karl entered the Teachers' Training College in Pasing, now a suburb of Munich, where he joined his brother Fritz; he remained there for three years.

In Frankfurt meanwhile, Hindemith returned from the barracks to his seat in the Opera pit, not even stopping to spend an evening with his mother, brother and sister. His relationship with the Rottenbergs developed steadily from this point. He was busy composing, completing the set of Six Sonatas, Op. 11, begun while still in uniform. Two of these were for violin with one each for viola and cello, all with piano accompaniment. The last, unusually, were for violin and for viola alone, following the precedent of some late works by Max Reger. Hindemith also produced two sets of songs, one to words by Walt Whitman in German translation, Op. 14, and a short one-act opera, *Mörder, Hoffnung der Frauen* ('Murder, Hope of Women'), using a highly symbolic, sadistic text by the Expressionist painter Oskar Kokoschka. The outdoor première of Kokoschka's short play had provoked a riot in Vienna in 1908. Hindemith was attracted to the play not because of its notoriety, but as an extreme example of Expressionism, the most vital avant-garde movement of the time. He had decided to compose an opera because the form appealed to him, rather than for a commission. On leave during July 1918, he had discussed a possible opera libretto with the sculptor Benno Elkan – later the librettist of Ernst Toch's *The Princess and the Pea* (1925) – and on his return home the next year, Hindemith found Frankfurt to be a leading centre of Expressionist study and discussion. He knew Kokoschka's work as both writer and painter from the periodical *Die Kunstblatt* ('Art News'). Kokoschka in turn was flattered and proud that his play had been set to music, but by all accounts never saw Hindemith's opera.

'Freedom lies in the freedom of one who thinks differently': Rosa Luxemburg, one of the leaders of the failed Berlin coup, brutally assassinated in November 1918

Hindemith went looking for two other suitable but contrasting texts to act as companions for *Mörder, Hoffnung der Frauen* to form a full-evening triple-bill. Although Kokoschka had written other plays, Hindemith decided on a short, amusing – and appropriately vulgar – one by Franz Blei. Hindemith's choice of text was by no means arbitrary, since he had decided that the three operas would deal, in varying ways, with the themes of violent sexuality and society's repression – even punishment – of it. *Das Nusch-Nuschi*, styled a 'play for Burmese marionettes', is a satirical affair in which a philanderer is castrated for his sins by the creature of the title, whose nonsense name literally translates as 'Nuts-Nuts' (in the colloquial sense of nuts for testicles). Unlike the intense and powerful *Mörder, Hoffnung der Frauen*, *Das Nusch-Nuschi*, which is over twice as long at a full hour, is a scherzo by comparison.

At Frankfurt Opera, Ludwig Rottenberg determined to be as enterprising as he could despite the political chaos, enabling Hindemith as *Konzertmeister* to encounter at first hand the operas *Fennimore and Gerda* by Frederick Delius, *Die Gezeichneten* ('The Stigmatized') by Frank Schreker and *Scheherazade* by his old composition teacher, Bernhard Sekles. The most unusual item presented was the posthumous production of what is probably the first science fiction opera, *Die ersten Menschen* ('The First Men') by Rudi Stephan, a former pupil of Sekles's at the Hoch Conservatory, who had been killed fighting on the Eastern front in 1915, aged twenty-eight. But by far the most important musical event of the year for Hindemith was the concert devoted entirely to his own music – the first ever – staged in Frankfurt. On 2 June, Emma Lübbecke-Job accompanied Hindemith on the piano in two of the recently completed sonatas, for violin and viola (Op. 11 Nos. 1 and 4). The composer appeared as violist again with the Rebner Quartet playing his First String Quartet, Op. 10; all five performers then combined to perform the Piano Quintet in E minor, written two years previously. On Sekles's suggestion, Hindemith hawked these pieces to a publisher, choosing Schott over Breitkopf and Härtel. B. Schott's Söhne were a local firm based in nearby Mainz but possessing a network of offices abroad, including London. They issued the First Quartet the very next month, starting an association which was to endure for the rest of Hindemith's life.

Colleagues were taken aback at Hindemith's cataloguing of his five sonatas as opus 11, a set instead of separate works. The Romantic Era had promulgated the notion that each composition or opus was a complete and inviolable work of art; Hindemith's invoking of the archaic Classical tradition of combining several like-intended works into an album was therefore irregular and prophetic of the 'back-to-Bach' movement that would become prevalent in the mid- to late-1920s.

While searching for a text to complete his trilogy of operas, Hindemith continued to produce music with astonishing ease, baffling his new publishers. A clutch of exploratory piano pieces appeared in late 1919 and 1920, mirroring and tracing his investigation of the Expressionist manner, most of which were never published. One of them was a sonata (listed as Op. 17 in Hindemith's own

Opposite, Oskar Kokoschka's lurid poster for the pre-war Viennese première of his play *Murder, Hope of Women*, which Hindemith set as a one-act opera in 1919

KOKOSCHKA
OK
DRAMA-KOMOEDIE
SOMMERTHEATER IN DER
KUNSTSCHAU
REGIE-ERNST REINHOLD
DRUCK VON ALBERT BERGER WIEN VIII. TIGERG. 17.

catalogue), actually turned down by Schott. The five *Dance Movements* of the following year followed a less experimental path. And while the Rebner Quartet successfully performed the First Quartet on several occasions, Hindemith wrote a more radical Second in C major.

In March 1920 an attempt was made by right-wing extremists to seize power under Wilhelm Kapp, causing Chancellor Ebert's government to flee from Berlin to Dresden. The putsch foundered after four days of popular protests including a strike which paralysed Berlin. Communist sympathizers in the Ruhr formed a Red Army which was suppressed by the pro-government Free Corps. There was a successful coup in Bavaria which consolidated that State's anti-left and anti-democratic orientation. Trouble continued into 1921, the worst instance being a second Communist-led coup attempt in March. Hindemith was able to ignore the unrest, since Frankfurt was not the centre of any particular militancy. Even the punitive occupation by French soldiers of several German cities – including Frankfurt, and nearby Darmstadt – in 1920 and again in 1923 provoked no interest on his part. By contrast Karl Amadeus Hartmann, undecided as to whether to pursue a career in music or follow his father and eldest brother into painting, was in these adolescent years exposed to political causes and effects at their most extreme in Munich, events which would colour both his conduct and his music in the difficult years to come.

3

Dancing on a Volcano 1920–33

Rebellion on the streets: Heinrich Himmler, future head of the Gestapo, raises the standard as the 'Beer Hall' putsch gathers momentum in Munich, 1923

The performance … represented a desecration of our artistic citadels. The content is of an indescribable vulgarity. Everything which to us is holy is here dragged through the mud in a spirit that is not German … How long will we Germans permit such things to be done to us?

Karl Grunsky, München *Abendzeitung*, after the 1921 première of Hindemith's opera *Das Nusch-Nuschi*

Dancing on a Volcano 1920–33

At the outset of 1921, Hindemith was essentially a local figure around Frankfurt and Mainz. By the end of the following year, he was known across the country as an *enfant terrible* of the ultra-modernist school.

He played on as *Konzertmeister* of Frankfurt Opera but, after returning from a concert tour of Holland and Spain, resigned from Rebner's old-fashioned quartet. His chief areas of interest were becoming more and more modern. This change of perspective was assisted by the arrival, late in 1920, of Wilhelm Furtwängler as director of the Museum Concerts. Furtwängler remained just one year but established a cordial and sympathetic rapport with Hindemith. It was under Furtwängler's direction that Arnold Schoenberg's major Expressionist symphonic poem, *Pelleas und Melisande* (1902–3), was performed in Frankfurt. In 1922, Furtwängler took over as artistic director of the Berlin Philharmonic Orchestra, being replaced by the yet more progressively minded Hermann Scherchen, who made an incalculable impact on the development and direction of European contemporary music over the next forty years.

Early in 1921 Hindemith finished the third of his short one-act operas, *Sancta Susanna*. This torrid work to a libretto by August Stramm concerned the nocturnal sexual fantasies of a novice nun. It was theatrical dynamite even by today's standards, and Fritz Busch flatly refused to première it in Stuttgart. Busch had no qualms about presenting both *Mörder, Hoffnung der Frauen* and *Das Nusch-Nuschi* and these proved to be quite scandalous enough. During the latter work's castration scene, Hindemith had quoted from Wagner's *Tristan und Isolde*; composer, conductor and orchestra were taken aback at the intensity of reaction the incident generated from Wagnerians in the audience, but the publicity did Hindemith no harm whatsoever. The following March, Hindemith's future father-in-law, Ludwig Rottenberg, presented the triple-bill complete, and created a second and more far-reaching sensation. Hindemith's attitude to these three operas changed, as he moved away from Expressionist precepts and by the end of the decade he began to view them as aberrant. In the 1930s, under the Nazi yoke, they were a great, almost dangerous, embarrassment to him.

Further controversy erupted at the first new music festival at Donaueschingen that summer over the première of his Second String Quartet, Op. 16. The work had been unsuccessfully submitted to the American benefactress of contemporary music, Elizabeth Sprague Coolidge; following its rejection Schott sent the work to the new festival without Hindemith's approval. The first he knew of the matter was when the Havemann Quartet refused to play it. Never one to miss out on an opportunity, Hindemith formed a new quartet with his brother Rudolf and the violinists Licco Amar (who at twenty-four had been appointed *Konzertmeister* of the Berlin Philharmonic Orchestra) and Walter Caspar. The Amar–Hindemith Quartet (later known more simply as the Amar quartet), born out of such necessity, became a by-word for progressive music-making for the rest of the decade. On 8 August 1922, their performance in Salzburg of Webern's Five Movements for String Quartet had to be abandoned when police were called in to break up a riot in the concert hall.

Above, Hindemith, the viola virtuoso, c. 1930; *right*, the front cover of Hindemith's Piano Suite, published in 1922

1922

SUITE FÜR KLAVIER

PAUL HINDEMITH

ED 1732

SCHOTT

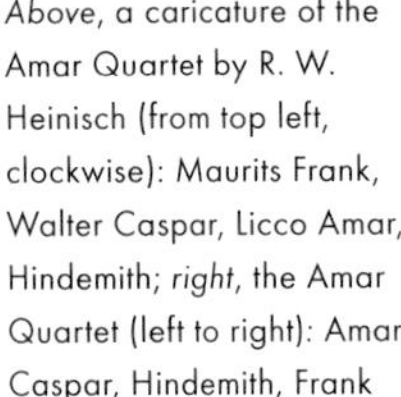

Above, a caricature of the Amar Quartet by R. W. Heinisch (from top left, clockwise): Maurits Frank, Walter Caspar, Licco Amar, Hindemith; *right*, the Amar Quartet (left to right): Amar, Caspar, Hindemith, Frank

It is not surprising that in such a restless and unstable country as Germany the arts should have reflected the turbulence of the streets and the widespread disaffection with the old order. Many creative figures were led to explore radical modes of expression and Hindemith was no exception in this respect. Alongside the operas and string quartets (a third, completed in 1921, raised critics' eyebrows by its lack of a key-signature) he was perfectly adept at producing dance-band arrangements at a moment's notice. He submitted several of these for Schott's consideration, but thought better of it immediately and most of them have disappeared. One spin-off was the orchestral *Well-Tempered Ragtime*, which takes as its main theme a fugue subject from Bach's collection, *The Well-Tempered Clavier*; another, on a larger scale, was *Kammermusik* No. 1: a four-movement suite for a small band including accordion, a canister of sand, and a siren. The Finale, entitled '1921', was written as a tribute to that year's Donaueschingen festival; its première there in 1922 was a sensation and in the following year Hindemith was invited to join the organizing committee. The anarchic streak in Hindemith's music continued well into 1923, with a concoction of militarist parodies for the Amar Quartet entitled *Minimax* – the Quartet even posed out of doors 'on parade' for a photograph, their instrument bows aslant their shoulders like rifles – and a subversive evocation for string quartet of Wagner's *Flying Dutchman* Overture as if played by complete incompetents.

The year 1922 was a compositional *annus mirabilis* for Hindemith. The sheer quantity and variety that he achieved is staggering: two complete song cycles and part of a third; *Kleine Kammermusik*, Op. 24 for wind quintet; the first movement of a never-finished chamber symphony; the Piano Suite '1922'; a half-hour-long ballet *Der Dämon* ('The Demon'), and music for a children's opera, *Tuttifäntchen*. Also, a new set of four sonatas, Op. 25, for unaccompanied viola, viola d'amore (which instrument he had only learned to play in the spring of this same year) with piano, unaccompanied cello and viola with piano respectively. No less impressive was the speed with which he produced work of such a consistent and high standard.

An example of his facility is provided by the two short song cycles which Hindemith grouped collectively as opus 23. Between 6 and 8 January he set three poems from a collection by Eduard Reinacher for female voice, two violas and two cellos lasting just over a quarter of an hour: *Des Todes Tod* ('The Death of Death'). In the following month he took just four days to create its slightly larger companion piece, a set of six songs to words by one of the most influential Expressionist poets, Georg Trakl, for alto, flute, clarinet and string quartet: *Die junge Magd* ('The Young Maiden'). The great critic and aesthete Theodor Adorno, born in Frankfurt and yet another pupil of Sekles at the Hoch Conservatory (and later of Alban Berg in Vienna), regarded these as two of Hindemith's finest and most important compositions. For two works so close in period, spirit and value their fates were oddly divergent. *Die junge Magd* was warmly received at the second Donaueschingen festival that summer (in the same concert as *Kammermusik* No. 1) and was published soon afterwards. *Des Todes Tod*, after a private première in Berlin on 22 January, was not put into print until 1953.

The majority of critics did not share Adorno's estimation of Hindemith. While his musicality was never really in doubt – at least as a performer – his compositional facility aroused reactions bordering on derision. Rottenberg's success with the operatic triple-bill only fuelled the fire, though several commentators had to admit ruefully that both music and subject matter were popular with the public. The operas also inspired imitation, not least from Krenek who, in the wake of his smash-hit opera, *Jonny spielt auf* ('Johnny Strikes Up'), in 1927 created a triple-bill of his own, albeit far less risqué in plot.

Hindemith had abandoned the styles of *Mörder, Hoffnung der Frauen, Das Nusch-Nuschi* and *Sancta Susanna* by the time of their complete première in March 1922. The Third String Quartet and *Kammermusik* No. 1 possess fitful traces of the language to come, but the iconoclastic side of his artistic personality was still dominant. One of his most uncompromising works was the virtuoso Second Sonata for Unaccompanied Viola, the first item of the opus 25 set. The fourth of its five movements, an astonishingly wild study in perpetual motion, was reputedly written in the buffet car of the train carrying Hindemith on his way to its first performance. Critics and audiences were provoked by the aggressive, contrapuntal style which made few concessions to established norms or the comfort of their ears. Younger musicians, though, were tremendously impressed. One such was the twenty-year-old Karl Amadeus Hartmann who heard this sonata played by its composer (as well as *Kammermusik* No. 1 and *Die junge Magd*) in the mid-1920s. He was 'violently moved by the youthful force of [Hindemith's] aggressive and witty *Kammermusik* No. 1', which contrasted starkly with the music on offer in Bavaria. In 1923 Hindemith produced his Clarinet Quintet, Op. 30; the raucous opening, with the clarinet and strings playing at the top of their registers, must have seemed like a slap in the face compared with the autumnal, romantic quintets of composers such as Brahms, Reger and Robert Fuchs. Despite being one of Hindemith's finest chamber compositions, this brilliant work was not published until 1955.

Hindemith's major creation of 1923 was his third song-cycle, *Das Marienleben* ('The Life of Mary'). The set, for female voice and piano, is a sequence of fifteen poems on the life of the Virgin by the visionary poet Rainer Maria Rilke. In *Das Marienleben*, all the elements of Hindemith's mature voice appeared for the first time, purged of the extremes of Expressionism and experimentation that had served him well until then. The sustained seriousness of tone (the cycle lasts about an hour-and-a-quarter) and consistently high quality of invention mark *Das Marienleben* out as a watershed in Hindemith's career; in many respects he was not the same composer on its completion as he had been at its conception.

Meanwhile, Germany's economic situation was reaching breaking point. When Germany defaulted on reparation payments, French and Belgian troops marched into the Rhineland and occupied the Ruhr industrial zone, remaining for two-and-a-half years. The government's acquiescence to this occupation precipitated states of emergency in several member republics, Bavaria leading the way. A separatist movement declared a republic in the Rhineland, which the French government, wanting a neutral 'buffer' between France and Germany, officially recognized in November 1923. This break-up of the country, apparently unopposed by the government, prompted the abortive 'Beer Hall' putsch in Munich, with General Ludendorff and Adolf Hitler at the head. Political turmoil led to the withdrawal of foreign investment and the collapse of the currency, which plummeted to 4.2 billion marks to the dollar. Savings and long-term assets became worthless; however, many of the poor benefited from hyperinflation since debts were eradicated almost overnight. The uneasy

Economic and political unrest in the Weimar Republic, as depicted in the woodcut *The Agitator* by Frans Masareel

The years 1923–4 saw Germany slide into a deepening crisis caused by hyperinflation. *Top*, the worthless currency; *right*, Adolf Hitler (in the centre) and Ludendorff (in military uniform and helmet, four to the right of Hitler) at the march-past of the Nazi paramilitary wing, the SA, in Nuremberg on the anniversary of the Siege of Sedan, 2 September 1923 collaboration between employers and the trade unions broke down as working days lengthened and industrial disputes flared. The unions, rendered impotent by events, lost members as their credibility in the workplace declined; many subsequently migrated to extremist political parties. The Rhineland Republic, which had precipitated so much trouble, expired in February 1924 when the disgruntled local populace burned down the seat of government sited in the town hall in Pirmasens.

The German currency became literally worthless. It was cheaper to wallpaper a room with banknotes than use them to buy wallpaper. Hindemith became acutely aware of his fragile financial circumstances and complained that Schott were not treating him fairly. A three-month wrangle was resolved through lawyers in early 1923 when Schott agreed to pay him a salary. This enabled Hindemith to resign as *Konzertmeister* of the Opera in order to devote himself full time to composition, and solo and quartet playing. He moved the family into the Kuhhirtenturm (Cowherd's Tower), a medieval bastion on the walls of Sachsenhausen on the outskirts of Frankfurt. It was here that *Das Marienleben* was finished, in the top storey that he took for his music room, his piano having been swung in by crane through a window. Hindemith resided in the tower for four years, but his mother and sister remained until being bombed out twice in 1943–4.

Hindemith seems to have been genuinely relieved that his publishers acceded to his demands and developed a convivial working relationship with the directors Ludwig and Willy Strecker. Nor did his resignation from the Opera in the least bit sour his relationship with the director, Ludwig Rottenberg. On 24 May of the following year, 1924, Hindemith became his son-in-law in a quiet ceremony during a brief stopover from the Amar Quartet's concert schedule. Because of his playing commitments the honeymoon was postponed until the summer, after the Donaueschingen festival at which Hindemith was officiating. Adolf Rebner had dubbed Hindemith a 'modern troubadour' years before, but the epithet became even more apposite in the mid-twenties. His activity was frenetic: with the Amar Quartet he gave 129 concerts (in some, giving solo performances of his own sonatas) in eighty-one cities in 1924 alone, still finding time to compose, get married and help run a major new music festival. Gertrud accepted his priorities without demur; she had absolute faith in his genius and adopted the roles first of personal assistant and years later, more proprietorially, of a kind of social manager, shielding him as best she could to allow him to work. Her devotion to Paul, much misunderstood, was tragically underlined by a miscarriage late in their first year together which left Gertrud permanently unable to conceive.

Hindemith's compositional haul kept on accumulating. After *Das Marienleben*, he embarked on his third collection of instrumental sonatas, grouped as opus 31 – two for unaccompanied violin, a third for viola alone and the delightful, miniature 'Canonic Sonatina' for two flutes. These were followed by the Piano Music with Orchestra, where the pianist uses his left hand only, the Clarinet Quintet, *Minimax* and the Fourth String Quartet Op. 32, a String Trio Op. 34, Six Motets for chorus, Op. 33, and a chamber piano concerto. This last was entitled *Kammermusik* No. 2 and with its two immediate successors from 1925, one each for cello and violin, the lithe, athletic style of his most typical music of the twenties and thirties was fully achieved. Hindemith once again ignored convention by grouping these concertos (like his sonatas) as a set, opus 36, to which he added a fourth item, the *Kammermusik* No. 5 for viola and large chamber orchestra, in 1927. Two further concertos, No. 6 for viola d'amore and No. 7 for organ, followed hard on the heels of No. 5 to complete the series.

Gertrud and Paul Hindemith in 1924, the year in which they were married

The idea of the chamber concerto, derived from the model of concerti grossi of the seventeenth and eighteenth centuries was much on Hindemith's mind during this period. Quite apart from his own *Kammermusik* pieces, he was involved as a juror in an international competition organized by Schott for new chamber concertos involving one or more solo instruments. Hindemith had few illusions about what might be achieved in such a competition beyond mere advertisement. Having by March 1925 looked over many of the 108 entries (submitted pseudonymously), he commented in a letter to Willy Strecker on the absence of really effective writing for the solo instruments and the unidiomatic use of the supporting ensembles. The result was something of a compromise. The first prize was shared between five composers: Paul Dessau, the Russian Alexander Tcherepnin, the Finn Aarre Merikanto, Ernst Toch and Hermann Wunsch (whose Fifth Symphony won the German section of the Columbia Graphophone Company's Schubert centenary competition). Later in 1925 Hindemith initiated a new form of composition – the concerto for orchestra. His pioneering example is an entertaining suite, a *Kammermusik* for full orchestra. There is little trace of the virtuoso writing for sections or individual instruments found in the more familiar concertos by Bartók and Witold Lutosławski.

The Cowherd's Tower, the Hindemith family home in Sachsenhausen from 1923

One of Hindemith's fellow jurors was Josef Haas, a Reger pupil who belonged to the so-called 'Munich' school of composers. His innate academicism left him out of sympathy with many developments in the 1920s, although this did not stop him playing an active part in the Donaueschingen Festivals. Haas taught composition at the State Academy in Munich, where from 1925 one of his pupils was Karl Amadeus Hartmann, who had left the Teachers' Training College at Pasing. After a period which included temporary work in an office, Hartmann prevailed over his parents' better judgement and was allowed to study music. Richard Hartmann had even locked the piano lid to deter his son from using it but, as part of the deal, Karl now undertook to learn an instrument in order to provide him with some sort of earning capacity. It is characteristic of his independence that he should have lit upon the trombone, not an obvious choice for a budding composer. For a time at the end of the 1920s, the State Opera in Munich employed him as a trombonist on a freelance, as required basis. His orchestral career was not a great success – too

Weimar Germany experienced an astonishing outburst of artistic activity, including Expressionist work such as the Einstein Tower, *above*, built in Potsdam in 1922 by Erich Mendelssohn often he missed his entries because he was busy listening to the rest of the orchestra. The death of Hartmann's father in 1925, aged fifty-nine, brought him still closer to his eldest brother, Adolf, who nurtured his talent, and provided much-needed financial support, especially in the perilous period of the Weimar Republic.

It was an unstable Germany into which Hans Werner Henze was born, the eldest of six children, on 1 July 1926. The year of his birth saw the publication of Hitler's *Mein Kampf* and the formation of the Hitler Youth (into which Henze would be forcibly enlisted in 1938). The economy was slowly recovering and a more optimistic climate was reflected in an artistic and cultural boom. The Bauhaus movement, led by the architect Walter Gropius, was revolutionizing the world of visual art, whilst on 10 February 1927, Krenek's jazzy opera, *Jonny spielt auf*, launched a new sensation.

Henze's father, Franz Gebhardt Henze, was born in Hanover in 1898. After the end of the First World War (in which he suffered head injuries, at Verdun) Franz Henze qualified as a teacher, married Margarete Adele Geldmacher, who was nine years his junior, and moved south to Westphalia to take a job in Gütersloh, where Hans was born. In 1929, the family moved to Bielefeld when Henze's father took up a new post. As Henze recalls, 'It was a modern school, with free education and was called "free school", with a modern system of education. The kids chose what they wanted to do, a little bit like in the anthroposophic Rudolf Steiner schools. It was a nice school, a nice job because it also meant a station upwards in his career.' In Bielefeld the family enjoyed a settled life and began to expand.

The new creative spirit found a fresh medium in the nascent art form of the cinema: *right*, a still from the Expressionist classic *Nosferatu* of 1922

The young Hans Werner Henze (left) and his brother Gerhard, at play in the early 1930s

Hindemith, by now at the height of his powers, was engaged on a new opera, bigger in scale than the three one-acters. After much searching, he decided upon E. T. A. Hoffmann's *Das Fräulein von Scuderi* ('The Lady of Scutari'). The libretto was written by Ferdinand Lion and concentrated on the character of Cardillac, a jeweller so besotted by his craft that he murders his customers to reclaim his work. In some ways, *Cardillac* is the most consistently impressive of all of Hindemith's operas, the action and the music fast-moving, the orchestration – requiring around forty players – crisp, and the subject intense without the excesses of the triple-bill. It met with a mixed response. Critics were on the whole rather cool, but musicians such as Hartmann and the conductor Otto Klemperer were bowled over. The music, Hartmann recalled, 'made a deep and lasting impression on me. I was overwhelmed by the bold and cool manner in which Paul Hindemith mixed a concert style into the music of the opera and was still able to effect a breathtaking stage performance.' An aspect of the opera's music derived from his instrumental pieces was the extended use of counterpoint throughout, the music moving horizontally in two or more compatible lines. Hindemith also restored – as did other composers independently at that time – several features from eighteenth-century opera, such as set-piece arias, duets, as well as adaptations of older instrumental forms such as the canon and passacaglia or chaconne.

Composing the music for his first full-length opera took barely two months. Having completed the *Konzertmusik*, Op. 41, for wind

Robert Burg (left) in the title role and Max Hirsel as the Officer in the première production of Hindemith's opera *Cardillac*, Dresden, November 1926

band immediately afterwards, Hindemith's ever-inquisitive mind became distracted by one of the odder fads of the 1920s: mechanical music. The principal and most popular instrument used was the pianola, or mechanical piano, whose keys were operated from inside by prepared piano rolls; the whole resembled a form of acoustic gramophone. Igor Stravinsky, one of Hindemith's greatest contemporaries, composed a few pieces for the pianola shortly after the Great War and several other composers experimented with it, particularly in regard to synchronizing music with silent film. Hindemith was sufficiently interested to feature mechanical instruments at the 1926 Donaueschingen Festival, composing on piano rolls a short dance piece, *Das triadische Ballett* ('The Triadic Ballet'). In collaboration with the Provençal composer Darius Milhaud, Hindemith experimented with synchronization of music with pictures, producing two film scores: *Felix the Cat at the Circus*, using a mechanical organ, in 1927 and *Vormittagspuk* ('Haunting in the Morning'), which used the pianola, a year later. Thereafter, Hindemith concentrated on purely acoustic instruments although he remained fascinated by exotic ones. Examples can be found in the Trio for Viola, Heckelphone and Piano of 1928 and the *Konzertstück* composed in 1931 for an early electronic instrument, the trautonium.

'In your greatness, you know everything': a cartoon by Willy Strecker, Hindemith's publisher, of the composer with conductor Otto Klemperer, 1926

The Donaueschingen Festival moved to bigger premises in Baden-Baden in 1927 and that year took advantage of the new facilities by adopting the additional theme of miniature operas, using chamber forces. Hindemith's own palindromic opera-sketch, *Hin und zurück* ('There and Back') was performed, as was the *Mahagonny* Singspiel by Kurt Weill and the brash young Socialist playwright, Bertolt Brecht, as well as Darius Milhaud's *L'Enlèvement d'Europe* ('The Rape of Europa'). *Hin und zurück* is one of Hindemith's most curious creations. The whole piece lasts less than fifteen minutes, the plot concerning a marital argument that leads to murder. At this point, action, text and music move into reverse, the opera unwinding like a film running backwards. In its contrived atmosphere and cinematic structure, *Hin und zurück* is quite unique amongst Hindemith's operatic output, although its use of palindrome would recur in *Ludus tonalis*. Hindemith's musical means may have already moved on from the highly charged manner of the triple-bill, but he still retained a preoccupation with 'modern' subjects; indeed, this was the most durable legacy of his dalliance with Expressionism. Of a violent cast, *Hin und zurück* was his third out of five operas to deal with murder; marital breakdown, a feature of both *Mörder, Hoffnung der Frauen* and *Hin und zurück*, would follow in *Neues vom Tage*; civil war in *Mathis der Maler*.

In February 1927 Hindemith was appointed professor of composition to postgraduates at the Hochschule für Musik in Berlin. Ever mindful of his own unorthodox and incomplete musical education, Hindemith explored and developed slowly his own method of instruction from first principles which would eventually bear fruit in his seminal treatise, *Unterweisung im Tonsatz* ('The Craft of Musical Composition'). By the end of the year he moved with Gertrud and a large model railway, his favourite pastime, to Berlin. Hindemith's mother and sister continued to reside in the Kuhhirtenturm in Sachsenhausen, where much of Hindemith's archive also remained, but Paul himself never returned to live in the tower.

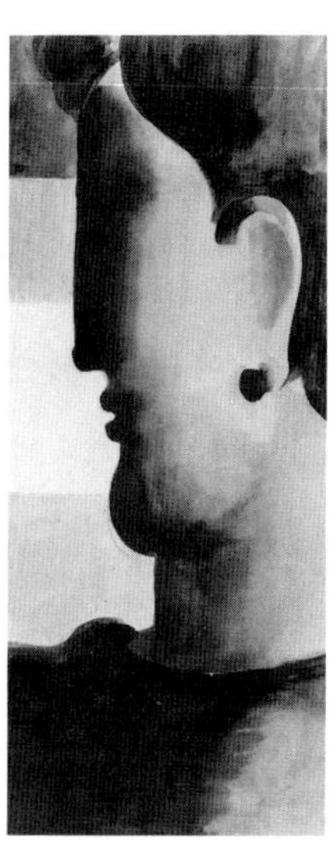

Oskar Schlemmer's *Symbolic Head*, c. 1922, was an image of calm created amidst artistic and political turmoil

Hand in hand with his official teaching, the main thrust of Hindemith's compositional output turned away from concert and theatrical works towards music that would be more accessible to amateur players. Several leading composers became involved in similar activities in other countries, not least Ralph Vaughan Williams in Britain and Heitor Villa-Lobos in Brazil. *Sing- und Spielmusik* ('Music to Sing and Play') was the collective title that Hindemith gave to the series of works written between 1927 and 1932, although these and many of his other works of the late 1920s and 1930s are often incorrectly referred to as *Gebrauchsmusik* (utility or functional music), a term Hindemith loathed. The official *Sing- und Spielmusik* comprises solos, duos, simple choral pieces as well as straightforward works for small orchestras, the cantata *Frau Musica* ('Lady Music') and a brief children's opera, *Wir bauen eine Stadt* ('Let's Build a Town'), written in collaboration with Berlin schoolchildren. Hindemith made allowances for the varying abilities of his intended performers by his flexibility with the instrumentation of some of - the larger pieces; wind instruments could be added if present to double vocal lines and some of the string parts were written to be played by beginners on open, unstopped strings without use of their left fingers. The climax of Hindemith's endeavours in this field came in 1932 with *Plöner Musiktag* ('Plön's Day of Music') in which he constructed a series of works for various times during the day. The sequence started with the *Morgenmusik* ('Morning Music') for brass – to be played from a tower early on – and ended with a short evening concert. Despite their educative purpose, some of these works have enjoyed considerable success and have entered the general repertoire in concert and on record, in particular the children's opera, a set of five pieces for string orchestra and the *Morgenmusik*. All are a tribute to Hindemith's ability to compose genuinely contemporary music without loss either of originality or quality and which still remained true to his own artistic standards.

As Hindemith was settling comfortably in Berlin as a teacher, Hartmann stormed out of the Academy in Munich after a series of disputes with his professors, notably Haas. 'I recognized the urgent need to master the composer's trade and was ready, even under difficult circumstances, to complete the necessary drilling. But when I had to submit some of my work to the Academy I saw that it would not get a good reception, so I did not bother the professors with it and let the door close firmly behind me', he wrote. Hartmann's enthusiasm for Stravinsky and Bartók strained his relationship with Haas, though he remained on cordial terms with his theory teacher, Gustav Geierhaas, and consulted him on an occasional basis over compositional problems.

Hartmann began to toy with different musical idioms and models, including jazz and Expressionism, until he met Hermann Scherchen, whose bold, committed advocacy of new music inspired the stylistically footloose young composer to find a personal path. Hartmann destroyed most of his early compositions and it is only possible to glimpse his early development during the 1920s through a handful of suites and sonatas mainly for solo piano (1924–6) and unaccompanied violin (1927). These reveal influences of Hindemith's piano music, neo-classicism and European notions of jazz. But in Hartmann's *Jazz Toccata and Fugue* for piano of 1928 it is Bartók's dark and heavily percussive style of piano writing that is brought to mind. The largest work of this period was the sequence of five miniature operas composed between 1929 and 1930, *Wachsfigurenkabinett* (loosely translatable as 'Wax Dolls' Display Case'; the rendering of 'Waxworks' or 'Waxworks Museum' carries the connotation of life-sized figures, rather than the dolls literally meant in the title).

Following page, Berlin pictured in the 1920s. In the early 1930s, when Hindemith was settled there, the turmoil was to increase. Everybody knew they were 'dancing on a volcano'.

RAMIKOS
Ernst Lauer
BLUMEN REIHER FEDERN
CAFE
Burgeff Grün
KONZERT
Cigarren
Loeser & Wolff

JOSETTI
76

All five operas have texts by a friend of Hartmann's, Erich Bormann, although the middle three have survived only in sketch form; in the 1980s they were brought into performable editions by the combined efforts of Günter Bialas, Wilfried Hiller and Henze. One of the set, which Hartmann completed, is *Leben und Sterben des heiligen Teufels* ('The Life and Death of the Holy Devil'). It centres on the Tsarina's mad monk, Rasputin, and received a workshop performance in 1929 at the Munich State Opera, under the auspices of the director, Clemens von Franckenstein, himself an operatic composer. His idea was to allow young composers to hear their operatic attempts – albeit with piano accompaniment – in reasonably proficient play-throughs. In 1930, a première of the whole set was announced in the magazine *Melos* at the State Theatre in Münster, but was abandoned for lack of money. Hartmann's attitude to these miniature operas became ambivalent. When Henze, as artistic director of a ballet company, wanted to mount *Die Witwe von Ephesus* as a dance-piece in 1949, Hartmann refused permission.

Hartmann organized a series of chamber concerts linked to the art exhibitions held by the *Juryfreien*, a Munich-based group of radical, anti-Establishment artists. The concerts featured contemporary progressive music to match the advanced style of the paintings and sculptures exhibited. In the five years up to 1933 the programmes included music by Béla Bartók, Conrad Beck, Alfredo Casella, Werner Egk, Alois Hába, Hindemith, Arthur Honegger, Darius Milhaud, Carl Orff, Maurice Ravel, Mátyás Seiber, Dmitry Shostakovich, Stravinsky and Ernst Toch. Several of Hartmann's own compositions received their first performances at these concerts, including the *Jazz Toccata and Fugue*, a sonatina and a sonata for piano, plus a *Toccata variata* for ten wind instruments, piano and percussion whose première on 6 March 1932 was conducted by Rudolf Hindemith. Hartmann himself directed a performance of Paul Hindemith's *Wir bauen eine Stadt* in 1932. A progressive link in German music thus began to cross the generations.

Hartmann met his future wife, Elisabeth, in 1929 when she was just sixteen years old and he was twenty-four. She was the daughter of Alfred Reussmann, the 'influential and prosperous general manager of a ball-bearing factory' in nearby Schweinfurt, and Adolf Hartmann was on friendly terms with Elisabeth's mother. When the renowned

Austrian tenor Julius Patzak appeared in Munich in Eugen d'Albert's opera *Tiefland* ('Lowlands'), Karl went to the Reussmanns' house to pick up Adolf's ticket and met Elisabeth. She was sent to England for a year, her father disapproving of their relationship as 'socially inappropriate', but they kept up a correspondence.

Hindemith began to find that teaching, playing and administration got in the way of composition. He started work on a full-scale opera, *Neues vom Tage* ('Today's News'), to a libretto by Marcellus Schiffer, a writer of cabaret revues with whom he had collaborated on *Hin und zurück*. This heavy-handed satire centred on the efforts of a couple, Eduard and Laura, to obtain a divorce; marital disharmony was a common operatic subject at this time, as is apparent from Schoenberg's high-minded *Von heute auf morgen* ('From Today Until Tomorrow'), Strauss's *Intermezzo*, and *Der gewaltige Hahnrei* ('The Magnificent Cuckold') by Berthold Goldschmidt. Hindemith gave full rein to his anarchic streak for the last time in a score that pokes fun at everything within its field of view, from operatic convention to museum guides. Act One opens with a 'hate duet' in which Eduard and Laura hurl abuse at each other over breakfast; later comes the 'kitsch duet' between Laura and 'handsome Herr Hermann', hired to provide her with grounds for divorce. The Second Act begins with a scandalous scene in which Laura, in the bath, sings of the joys of hot water; by the final act the still-unresolved divorce action itself becomes the subject of a cabaret revue. The initial Berlin production was conducted by Otto Klemperer at the Kroll Opera (he had successfully presented *Cardillac* the year before) but flopped; only when Arthur Rabenalt, who had mounted an acclaimed production in Darmstadt, was brought in did it become a hit. Critical reaction, including Adorno's, was dismissive: one critic wrote that while 'one part of the audience seemed honestly to enjoy themselves ... the rest were so appalled that they were unable to compose themselves enough to boo'. Rather more sinisterly, Hindemith offended some powerful sensibilities: Hitler and Goebbels attended a performance and left in disgust at the sight of a naked soprano bathing on stage.

Hindemith's other major work of 1929 landed him in more immediate hot water. The cantata *Badener Lehrstück vom Einverständnis* ('Baden's Lesson on Consensus', known generally just as *Lehrstück*) was written for the Baden-Baden Festival to a ponderously moralistic

text provided by the militant Socialist writer Bertolt Brecht and started out as a culmination of the *Music to Sing and Play* series. The intention was that the audience would join in communal singing of the hymn-like numbers. Hindemith was not concerned about the shock value of Brecht's text, which features the dismemberment of the 'important person', Herr Schmidt, by a brace of clowns in order to cure him of his ailments. The scene called for minimal music, a raucous, circus-style march used to accompany the lopping-off of Herr Schmidt's foot, leg, ear, arm and head. The audience at Baden-Baden on 28 July 1929, was appalled. The celebrated violinist Carl Flesch, a regular performer at Baden-Baden, recorded his reactions in a letter to a friend dated 4 August 1929:

I am of the opinion that extreme judgements – 'very good' or 'very bad' – are entirely out of place here. It is an experiment that so far has not entirely come off. On the positive side we have the active involvement of the audience; on the negative, the enormous pretension with which the libretto is spewing platitudes as if they were evangelical revelations ... Brecht is to be envied for his conceited effrontery with which he presents ... apparently alcohol-drenched literary pranks as divine inspirations. Due to the opposition aroused thereby even in the most unprejudiced listener, you can't do justice to the music, because you don't gain any clear impression of it.

Left, the 'agent provocateur' Bertolt Brecht, librettist of Hindemith's 'scenic cantata' *Badener Lehrstück*, 1929–30. *Right*, front cover of the vocal score of Hindemith's 1928 opera *Neues vom Tage*; the scene featuring the unclothed heroine in a bath outraged Hitler and Goebbels during the 1930 Kroll Opera production in Berlin.

Lehrstück appeared in the final concert at Baden-Baden; from 1930, the experimental festival had to be transferred to Berlin, by which time composer and librettist were at loggerheads. Brecht had been immensely pleased over the furore and happy enough with Hindemith's contribution. The composer had also helped out Brecht's usual collaborator, Kurt Weill, by rapidly producing six numbers (out of sixteen) for the cantata *Der Lindberghflug* ('Lindbergh's Flight') in order to meet the deadline for a première at Baden-Baden the day before *Lehrstück*. Hindemith, in the wake of the controversy, high-handedly instructed Schott to omit the controversial Herr Schmidt scene from future performances. Nobody consulted Brecht who, not surprisingly, was furious. The two men were never reconciled: plans for an opera evaporated and Weill replaced Hindemith's numbers for *Der Lindberghflug* with his own. *Lehrstück* was placed under an interdict by Brecht which virtually prevented it being heard for three decades.

In order to gain sufficient time to complete *Neues vom Tage* and undertake other commissions that were coming in, Hindemith left the Amar Quartet but continued to give solo performances and struck up a trio partnership with the violinist Josef Wolfsthal and cellist Emanuel Feuermann. One notable solo event was his première at short notice of the concerto that William Walton had written for the leading English violist, Lionel Tertis, who had rejected it. The appearance of Hindemith, an acknowledged celebrity, in a new British work did much for his public image in London. In Germany, his triumph was eclipsed by the sudden death on the same day, 3 October 1929, of the foreign minister and elder statesman of the Weimar Republic, Gustav Stresemann.

With hindsight, the death of Stresemann, who had briefly been Chancellor in 1923, marked the high-water mark of the Weimar Republic culturally, economically and politically. Had he lived, it is doubtful he could have steered the vulnerable state through the chaos of the Wall Street Crash and the ensuing world-wide depression. The fragile recovery was destroyed, unemployment began to soar and the country plunged into deepening crisis, with governments coming and going and fighting breaking out sporadically in the streets. Berlin from 1930 onward became a dangerous place to be, although still a magnet culturally. The young Danish composer, Vagn Holmboe,

President Hindenburg with Konrad Adenauer, then Bürgermeister of Cologne and future President of postwar West Germany, in a motorcade in 1926

travelled there in 1930 in order to study with Hindemith at the Hochschule. However, Hindemith was abroad on tour and the vetting committee apparently considered the pieces Holmboe showed them too atonal and he was refused admission. His future wife, the Romanian pianist Meta Graf, was a Hindemith pupil and over the next three years Holmboe regularly visited Berlin. He recalls: 'The years in Berlin 1930–33 were hectic. Everybody knew that they were "dancing on a volcano". Lots of concerts with the best conductors (before they flew away to safety), theatre, exhibitions, etc., etc. The streets were not safe, Nazi and Communist shootings were a normal thing in the northern part of the city – at the same time, there was this enormous supply of music.'

As ever, Hindemith responded to the political turbulence by ignoring it. No trace of upheaval or crisis will be found in *Wir bauen eine Stadt* or the three *Konzertmusiks*, for viola and large chamber orchestra, Op. 48; piano, brass and two harps, Op. 49; and string orchestra and brass, Op. 50 – the last composition to which he assigned an opus number – which all date from 1930. The *Konzertmusik* for viola was written for himself as soloist (although dedicated to Darius and Madeleine Milhaud) and was first performed in Hamburg on 28 March with Wilhelm Furtwängler conducting. The two other *Konzertmusik*s were both written to American commissions, but Hindemith had no intention of travelling to America to hear them, even though his old friend Emma Lübbecke-Job was the pianist at the première of *Konzertmusik* for piano, brass and two harps in Chicago.

Throughout 1931 Hindemith worked on what would prove to be his largest non-operatic work: the oratorio *Das Unaufhörliche* ('The Perpetual') to a text provided by another politically opinionated writer, Gottfried Benn. Hindemith may have chosen the right-winger Benn to spite Brecht; at the height of the *Lehrstück* affair he had heard Benn get the better of Brecht in a radio debate. By the end of 1931 he had completed the huge oratorio on a similar scale to the Bach Passions and Beethoven's *Missa Solemnis. Das Unaufhörliche* failed to make much impression; it has never entered the repertoire, probably because of its size rather than quality, for it is a moving and beautifully crafted score, with a nobility of utterance that was quite new in Hindemith's output. The oratorio also lacked the scandal-value that Berlin audiences had come to expect after *Neues vom Tage* and *Lehrstück*, although some material from the latter, including the 'dismemberment' march, was recycled within it. Perhaps it appeared at the wrong time: 1930s Berlin was in no mood for a grand symphonic synthesis. It demanded thrills, musical quick-fixes. Hindemith began to toy with the idea for a new opera, but by the end of 1932 had still not settled finally on the right subject.

Hartmann's output began to accelerate. In 1931 he produced several small-scale works on broadly Hindemithian lines, often with unconventional instrumentation. These included a *Dance Suite* for clarinet, bassoon, trumpet, horn and trombone, *Burleske Musik* for piano, wind and percussion – dedicated to Elisabeth – and the *Kleines Konzert* for string quartet and percussion. He tried his hand at three concertos: for trumpet (later revised as the Fifth Symphony), for cello (lost) and a triple concerto – also referred to as *Symphonie-Divertissement* – for bassoon, trombone and double bass which he seems not to have completed. Hartmann was now ready to tackle pure orchestral music in the grand manner.

Opposite, the growing menace institutionalized: the Nazis, the largest single political party in Germany, at a rally in 1929

That summer the political situation within Germany had become increasingly tense. After a rapprochement between Hitler and Chancellor von Papen in June, the government lifted the ban on the Nazi paramilitary wings, the SA and SS. Taking this as carte blanche to act with a free hand, by mid-July Nazi activists were holding pitched battles in the streets of Berlin with their rival Communist gangs, forcing the government to effect reprisals. But the unrest spiralled out of control, spreading to other cities such as Hamburg and Dresden and, in December, even to the Parliament building – the Reichstag – itself. Then on 30 January, Hitler was appointed Chancellor; the Third Reich had begun.

4

The Wellspring of Artistic Intuition 1933–9

Members of the Hitler Youth exercise with their standards, the 'emblems of might'

Strauss asked what would happen if every Jewish Kapellmeister in Germany departed. I said I thought things would turn out all right, whereupon Frau Strauss said, in her strong dialect: 'Well, if they do anything to you, just come and see me!' Strauss, who was sitting on the sofa smiling broadly, commented: 'Oh, yes, this would be just the moment to stick your neck out for a Jew!'

Otto Klemperer, *Minor Recollections*, 1964

The Wellspring of Artistic Intuition 1933–9

Opposite, 'Triumph of the Will': a Nazi party rally at Nuremberg, 1935

The Nazi party, or National Socialist German Worker's party, never secured an outright electoral victory. By 1932, however, they had become the largest single party in the German parliament. The 'Brown Shirts' – as they were known from their paramilitary uniforms – enjoyed popular support at all levels of German society despite their persistent deployment of terror tactics. Adolf Hitler was therefore a leading candidate for the chancellorship but only reached office after the Nazis' vote had fallen by two million at the polls in 1932. The ageing President Hindenburg believed that this electoral setback would enable him to control Hitler, but once in power the Nazis rapidly effected a stranglehold on the country. By mid-July Germany had become a one-party State – and when Hindenburg died the next year Hitler abolished the presidency. Yet, in spite of the ruthlessness of their totalitarian regime and the ensuing catastrophe of the Holocaust, the Nazi administration was often chaotically inefficient. Hitler encouraged a situation where different spheres of action overlapped, forcing rival ministers into competition, and departments of State ensured that the government depended primarily on his patronage. This generated intense rivalry in artistic affairs, where Joseph Goebbels and his 'Ministry of Propaganda and Enlightenment' were at odds with Alfred Rosenberg's cultural department, the Kulturgemeinde, and with Hermann Goering's lordship over the capital. Hindemith found himself repeatedly at the mercy of this inter-departmental strife.

The Nazis' racial hatred towards Jews and other 'non-Aryan' ethnic groups found early expression, and attempts were made to implement it systematically. At first these were not always successful: a boycott of Jewish shops in April 1933 had to be abandoned after just one day because the precarious economy could not stand the shock. Discrimination in employment was more effective, however. Arnold Schoenberg and Franz Schreker, two of the country's most important teachers and composers, were summarily dismissed from their posts

Following page, 'The Saar is free. Hail to the Führer!' Germany formally reoccupies the Saarland without opposition, 1935

N·S·D·A·P·

Die
Heil
Reichsbahn

st frei.
führer!

President, Chancellor and henchman (left to right): Hitler, Hindenburg and Hermann Goering, 1933

in Berlin, as were hundreds of lesser figures, several of them close colleagues or friends of Hindemith. The purges of non-Aryans included Bernhard Sekles in Frankfurt; Kurt Weill, Artur Schnabel and Otto Klemperer in Berlin; Bruno Walter in Leipzig, Fritz Busch in Dresden. In early 1934 the school where Franz Henze was teaching was closed because its progressive, independent attitudes did not accord with Nazi party dogma. As Henze recalls: 'The young teachers were dispersed all over the place in little villages where they could be buried for good. The director of the school was arrested and was taken to a concentration camp where he stayed until the end of the war. When he came back he was made the Mayor of Bielefeld by the British.' Franz Henze and his family moved to Dünne, near the cigar-making town of Bünde. There he taught at the local village school and, according to his son, 'in no time – not more than a year – under the influence of three other teachers there who were wearing the brown uniforms', he was bullied into the party.

The flight of talent and ability caused by the Nazis' ethnic cleansing denuded Germany of a substantial proportion of its creative community. Thousands of musicians fled into exile, among them

Hindemith's friends, the violinists Licco Amar and Bronislaw Hubermann, wiping out at a stroke Germany's dominance in the interpretation of orchestral music. As the exodus proceeded, standards of performance fell embarrassingly. Not until the 1950s was the situation partially (but never fully) recovered. Some composers who remained were targeted by association. Krenek's music was banned in 1933 because the Nazis incorrectly assumed – on the evidence of his name – that he was a Czech of non-German origin. Productions of his opera *Jonny spielt auf* had anyway been disrupted by violent Nazi demonstrations for its 'Negro cultural associations'. Alban Berg and Anton von Webern, neither of them Jewish, were tainted as modernists and pupils of Schoenberg. In general, the music of composers the Nazis disapproved of, for whatever reasons, was liable to be labelled atonal, un-German and therefore degenerate. At a cultural rally in Düsseldorf in 1935, Rosenberg stated that the 'whole atonal movement is contradictory to the rhythm of blood and soul of the German nation'.

The perverted reasoning behind the Nazi artistic doctrines was made explicit in a speech that Adolf Hitler gave just seven weeks after entering office, on the day the infamous Enabling Law – granting him special plenipotentiary powers – was passed in the Reichstag: 'The world of bourgeois passivity is dispersing rapidly. Passionately

The Nazi-inspired book burnings of Jewish and 'degenerate' literature, 1933

the Heroic rises up as the future moulder of and leader of the destinies of nations. It is the task of Art to lend expression to this all-pervading Spirit of the Age ... blood and race are to be the wellspring of artistic intuition.' Yet the decimation of music became an embarrassment to the Nazi government, who were keen to use the arts to promote Germany's image abroad. Hindemith, whose wife was half-Jewish by blood but Lutheran by religion (and whose brother-in-law Hans Flesch was carted off to Oranienburg concentration camp in August 1933), could not be faulted as an 'Aryan'. But his music had incensed Hitler personally and was attacked by Nazi fanatics as being 'infected by Jewish intellectualism'. Goebbels accused him, quite incorrectly, of being an atonal composer; Stravinsky and Hartmann were similarly castigated. Because the government used a political slide-rule for defining atonality, the situation developed where Nazi-approved composers continued to compose in an atonal or twelve-note idiom. Winfried Zillig, who enjoyed equal success as a conductor and composer, was known to have been a pupil of Schoenberg's yet his music fooled the ideologues. The Danish composer, Paul von Klenau, even successfully defended the twelve-note method in the journal, *Die Musik*, in 1935 (omitting any references to Schoenberg), claiming that it was compatible with National Socialist principles.

Hindemith's attitude to these developments was ambivalent. He carried on teaching, the dismissals around him provoking no protest, and he affected to work with the replacements as if his Jewish ex-colleagues had left of their own accord. As with many Germans who were not politically active, Hindemith may have misjudged the Nazis to be a temporary phenomenon. The Jewish composer Berthold Goldschmidt recalls that Hindemith advised him to stay put – 'They are idiots, they won't last.' Even the attacks on his music did not elicit much response, partly because the works usually cited as examples of his un-Germanness were often those that he had private reservations about, such as the triple-bill and the Piano Suite '1922'. A successful revival of *Das Nusch-Nuschi* in Antwerp in March 1933, while Hindemith was there for the première of his Second String Trio, did not help matters. His few concert engagements in 1933 and 1934 were mostly outside Germany, with his Jewish partners Szymon Goldberg (who had replaced Josef Wolfsthal in the trio in 1931) and Feuermann, notably in Brussels, Vienna, Copenhagen and London, where Hindemith made his first gramophone recordings away from the Amar Quartet, composing in a few hours a little Scherzo for viola and cello as a fill-up for the final disc.

Hindemith had always displayed an ability to put aside outside events in order to pursue his muse and for much of 1933 his mind was elsewhere dealing with the more pressing matter of the new opera, his eighth. He had decided on using the Renaissance painter generally known by the name of Matthias Grünewald as the central character. This idea had originated with Willy Strecker but Hindemith initially turned it down, toying with at least two other subjects (one on the history of railways). Even before settling the libretto, which he wrote himself, Hindemith began to compose music for both the opera, which he entitled *Mathis der Maler* ('Mathis the Painter'), and an orchestral work, the latter to fulfil a commission from Furtwängler for the Berlin Philharmonic. He drew inspiration from Grünewald's great series of paintings for the altar of the monastery at Isenheim in Alsace. The subjects of these pictures include a concert of angels, the entombment of Christ and episodes in the life of St Anthony, the monastery's patron saint. For the angelic concert Hindemith made use of an old German folk-song, *Es sungen drei Engel ein'n süßen Gesang* ('Three Angels Sang a Sweet Song'). This became both the overture to the opera and the first movement of the orchestral work, where it yielded to a quiet interlude based on the final scene of the opera. Hindemith was unsure of the latter's use in the concert extract and for a time considered delivering just two movements to Furtwängler. The virtuoso finale he finally produced drew on two of Grünewald's St Anthony pictures and ended with a series of exhilarating 'Alleluias' for the full brass section. Inadvertently, he had produced his first symphony and cannot have known that it would prove to be his most enduringly popular score. Furtwängler was delighted, directing the symphony's première to great acclaim, critical and public, on 12 March 1934 and the composer himself conducted it for the German record company Telefunken shortly afterwards.

Two weeks prior to the première of the *Mathis der Maler* symphony, Hindemith had been invited to conduct his *Konzertmusik* for strings and brass at a concert of music by Nazi-approved composers, sharing the billing with Paul Graener, Siegmund von Hausegger, Hans Pfitzner and the president of the Reichsmusik-kammer, Richard

Trouble at home, acclaim abroad: *above*, Hindemith in Boston during his successful first tour of the United States, 1937; *right*, 'The Hindemith Case': Furtwängler's spirited but misguided defence of the composer in November 1934, which prompted a vitriolic response from Goebbels (see p. 87); *far right*, Hindemith at Ankara Conservatory (which he set up at the request of the Turkish government), with the Czech microtonal composer, Alois Hába.

Reichs-Ausgabe

Deutsche A

Berlin, 25. November 1934 (Sonntag) •

The Hindemith Case

By Wilhelm Furtwängler

Inasmuch as a short time ago, speaking at the meeting of the Reichsmusikkammer, the leader Reichsmusikerschaft (State Organization of Musi Prof. Dr. h. c. Gustav Havemann, mentioned the growing hostility towards the composer Hindemith, we are giving space today to the foll statements by Staatsrat Dr. Wilhelm Furtwängle

In certain circles a campaign against Paul Hindemith is being based on the thesis that he is "not acceptable" in the new Ger Why? Of what does one accuse him?

If one were to sketch a portrait of the composer Hindemith basis of these early works—to which should be added man ones, such as the Marienleben—one would be obliged to p him, whose blood is also purely Germanic, as an outspokenl man type. German in the high quality and straightforwardr his solid craft as in the chastity and restraint of his relativel outbreaks of emotion. The latest work of his to appear, the phony from the opera "Mathis der Maler", has only confirm impression.

It was his intellectual honesty that kept him from joining the ner succession. But the kind of text that corresponds to his, mith's, true nature can be seen in the only one which he hims written—namely, that of his recently-completed opera "Mat Maler". Nobody who reads it can overlook—among many things—the deep ethical quality which inspired its creatc enemies speak of an about-face, opportunism, etc. Quite apar the fact that Hindemith is the last person capable of such ac is quite impossible in the case of this work, which was begu before the national revolution.

One thing is certain: no other composer of the young gen has done more for the status of German music throughout the than Paul Hindemith. Furthermore, one cannot foresee toda importance his works may have in the future. But that is r point of this discussion. It is less a question of the "Hin case" than one of general principle. And what is more—th point on which we must be clear: we cannot afford, in the the present world shortage of truly productive musicians, pense light-heartedly with a man like Hindemith.

Einzelpreis 20 Pfennig

ne Zeitung

• 73. Jahrgang 25. 11. • Nr. 549-550 20 Pfennig

Der Fall Hindemith

Von

Wilhelm Furtwängler

Nachdem unlängst der Führer der Reichsmusikerschaft, Prof. Dr. h. c. Gustav Havemann, im Rahmen der Berliner Landestagung der Reichsmusikkammer den in letzter Zeit um sich greifenden Anfeindungen gegen den Komponisten Paul Hindemith öffentlich begegnet ist, geben wir heute den folgenden Ausführungen von Staatsrat Dr. Wilhelm Furtwängler Raum.

In gewissen Kreisen ist ein Kampf gegen Paul Hindemith eröffnet worden, mit der Begründung, daß er für das neue Deutschland „nicht tragbar" sei. Warum? Was wirft man ihm vor?

Wenn man nach diesen ersten Werken — zu denen auch aus späterer Zeit noch so manches zu rechnen wäre (z. B. das „Marienleben") — ein Bild des Komponisten Hindemith zu umreißen versuchte, müßte man ihn, der ja auch blutsmäßig rein germanisch ist, als einen ausgesprochen „deutschen" Typus bezeichnen. Deutsch in seiner schlicht handwerklichen Gediegenheit und gerade kernhaften Art ebenso wie in der Keuschheit und Zurückhaltung seiner relativ seltenen Gefühls-Ausbrüche. Das letzte bisher von ihm erschienene Werk, die Sinfonie aus der Oper „Mathis der Maler", hat diesen Eindruck von neuem bestätigt.

waren. Es war seine Ehrlichkeit, die ihn von einer Wagner Nachfolge abhielt. Wie aber ein Text aussieht, der seiner, Hindemiths, wirklicher Natur entspricht, zeigt der einzige Opern Text, den er sich selbst schrieb, der Text zu seiner letzten, erst vor kurzem beendeten Oper „Mathis der Maler". Niemand, der ihn liest, wird, — neben allem andern, — gerade das tiefe Ethos verkennen können, das seinen Schöpfer beseelt. Die ihn anfeinden, reden von Umstellung, Wahrnehmung der Konjunktur usw. Ganz abgesehen davon, daß Hindemith der letzte wäre, der dazu fähig ist, ist das bei diesem Werk schon deshalb nicht möglich, weil dessen Anfänge lange vor der nationalen Revolution liegen.

Sicher ist, daß für die Geltung deutscher Musik in der Welt keiner der jungen Generation mehr getan hat als Paul Hindemith. Im übrigen ist es heute natürlich nicht abzusehen, welche Bedeutung das Werk Hindemiths einmal für die Zukunft haben wird. Das ist es aber auch gar nicht, was hier zur Diskussion steht. Es handelt sich hier, vielmehr noch als um den besonderen „Fall Hindemith", um eine allgemeine Frage von prinzipiellem Charakter. Und weiter noch — auch darüber müssen wir uns klar sein: wir können es uns nicht leisten, angesichts der auf der ganzen Welt herrschenden unsäglichen Armut an wahrhaft produktiven Musikern, auf einen Mann wie Hindemith so ohne weiteres zu verzichten.

Strauss. Hindemith's work was generally well received despite the odd hiss, but officially all seemed well. In May, he moved to the Baltic coast to start work on the opera proper, and to celebrate his tenth wedding anniversary. The following month the conductor Hans Rosbaud was refused permission to perform the *Mathis der Maler* symphony for Frankfurt Radio. The grounds given were that while playing in Switzerland Hindemith had allegedly made defamatory remarks about the Führer. The ban on his music was never officially proclaimed, but this did not prevent the press, under Goebbels' instigation, from mounting a vitriolic onslaught against Hindemith. In November 1934, Hindemith threatened emigration if the attacks did not stop. The situation eased, to the extent that Johannes Schüler was able to perform the symphony in Essen on 20 November, but a boycott of Hindemith's music was then announced by Rosenberg's semi-official Kulturgemeinde. Furtwängler, who wanted to conduct the première production of the *Mathis der Maler* opera in Berlin, was incensed and wrote a front-page article, 'The Hindemith Case', in support of the composer, which appeared in the last liberal daily newspaper, the *Deutsche allgemeine Zeitung*. Furtwängler realized that the stated reasons for the latest attacks on Hindemith, such as his associations with Licco Amar, Goldberg and Feuermann, were not the real ones, lying 'in those of his works which are open to criticism from an ideological point of view, in particular on the grounds of certain of the texts he has chosen to set to music. It must be conceded that the libretti of the three one-act operas … are extremely dubious. The same applies to the *Badener Lehrstück* and *Neues vom Tage* – which is little more than a revue.' Of the triple-bill, Furtwängler continued: 'one may well ask whether their subject matter is in any way more perverse than that, say, of … Richard Strauss's *Salome*. And who is prepared to turn his back on Strauss because of the libretto of *Salome*?' Furtwängler then praised the 'profound sense of moral commitment' in the libretto of *Mathis der Maler* as well as the music of the symphony. Furtwängler's artistic case thus far had been even-handed and well-argued, yet publication made matters infinitely worse. The trouble lay in its final two paragraphs, where the conductor dared to question the government's right to censure the composer. Having pointed out that 'Hindemith has never engaged in political activity', Furtwängler posed the question, 'Where will it lead if we begin to apply the methods of political denunciation to art?' He concluded, 'It is less a question of the "Hindemith case" than one of general principle … we cannot afford … to dispense light-heartedly with a man like Hindemith.' In daring to speak out against Rosenberg, Furtwängler unwittingly drove Goebbels to his rival's defence in a much publicized reply, 'Why advance laurels for musical opportunist Hindemith?' Furtwängler was relieved of all his official posts and placed in limbo for eight months before he made his peace with Goebbels. In the meantime, the pressure was stepped up on the beleaguered composer: on 6 December he was attacked in a speech by Goebbels at a Nazi rally and further odium was heaped upon him in the press, not least by Rosenberg himself who termed Hindemith's compositions 'the foulest perversion of modern music'. By the end of the month Hindemith took, by mutual agreement, a six-month leave of absence from the Hochschule, in order to lie low and complete his opera.

Mathis der Maler, despite its setting during the Peasants' Wars and its central theme of the artist at odds with his world, is by no means a political opera. Nor was it – as some commentators found it expedient to claim – an allegory of the composer's experiences at the hands of the Fascist regime, since the libretto was substantively complete before the publication of Furtwängler's article. The music's noble high-mindedness placed it in direct descent from *Das Unaufhörliche* and was a logical consequence of the historical subject matter; as the oratorio remained almost completely unknown it seemed to be of sharper contrast to his previous work than in fact the opera was. Rather, music and composer were political victims; the vilification Hindemith suffered at the hands of Goebbels and Rosenberg was not inspired by the opera itself, but by their perceptions of its creator and his past record. Hindemith made no attempt to portray or satirize the Nazis musically (as it would later be claimed that other composers – such as Werner Egk in *Peer Gynt* – had done). His opera also lacked the political cutting edge of *Des Simplicius Simplicissimus Jugend* ('The Youth of Simplicius Simplicissimus') which Hartmann composed in secret during 1934–5.

In 1935 Hindemith received an unexpected invitation to establish a musical academy in Ankara. The Turkish authorities were impressed with Hindemith's practical method and his proposals. The Nazis, not

Vom Wahren und Falschen in der Kunst.

Die Rede des Führers und Reichskanzlers auf der Kulturtagung in Nürnberg.

Viel wichtiger bleibt demgegenüber die Stellungnahme unseres eigenen Volkes. Denn seine Anteilnahme oder Ablehnung ist die allein für uns als gültig anzusehende Beurteilung der Richtigkeit unseres kulturellen Schaffens. Und ich will dabei einen Unterschied machen zwischen dem Volk, das heißt, der gesunden blutvollen und volkstreuen Masse der Deutschen und einer unzuverlässigen, weil nur bedingt blutgebundenen dekadenten sogenannten „Gesellschaft". Sie wird manchesmal gedankenlos als „Oberschichte" bezeichnet, während sie in Wirklichkeit nur das Auswurfergebnis einer blutmäßig und gedanklich kosmopolitisch infizierten und damit haltlos gewordenen gesellschaftlichen Fehlzüchtung ist.

Of the True and the False in Art

Address by the Führer and Chancellor of the Reich at the Cultural Congress in Nürnberg

Much more important is the attitude of our own people. For its approval or rejection is for us the sole means of judging the rightness of our cultural creation. And here I should like to distinguish between the folk—that is to say, the healthy, full-blooded and patriotic masses of Germans—and an unreliable and (because the blood-ties are only partial) decadent so-called "society". This is often referred to thoughtlessly as the "upper crust", whereas it is in reality only the intellectually anemic, infected, cosmopolitan, socially unstable dregs resulting from faulty breeding.

'Of the True and the False in Art': Hitler voices his opinion in his address at the party congress in Nuremberg, 1934

wishing to displease an old ally, rehabilitated him at the Hochschule and released whatever material he required for the Turkish project. Hints were dropped about possible performances of his music, though his premières now only occurred abroad. The most important was his third and final viola concerto, *Der Schwanendreher* ('The Swan-Turner'), based on old German folk-songs. It was conducted in Amsterdam on 14 November 1935 by Willem Mengelberg, Hindemith's former antagonist in Frankfurt. By a further twist, Mengelberg – also conductor at the première of Hindemith's Violin Concerto five years later, shortly before the occupation of Holland – was temperamentally pro-Fascist.

Owing to the death of King George V in January 1936, the British première of *Der Schwanendreher* was cancelled at the last moment. In under six hours Hindemith dashed off an eloquent *Trauermusik* ('Mourning Music') for viola and strings for a broadcast the next night. Characteristically, Hindemith had time to construct the solo part in such a way that it could be played equally comfortably on the violin or cello. Although reported in the German press, neither this triumph for German music nor further trips to Ankara (where Béla Bartók was also now working) altered his situation. The Nazis' attitude to Hindemith remained inconsistent. In 1936, when performers were ministerially reprimanded for playing his music, the

**Dr. Goebbels
at the Annual Rally
of the Reichskulturkammer**

If the musical youth of Germany acknowledges the atonal musicians, that is just another proof of how necessary it is to combat (this tendency) relentlessly. We, for our part, can discover in it neither a way forwards nor the seeds of any future development ; we resist most energetically the tendency to regard this kind of artist as German and see in the fact of his blood-pure German origin only a practical proof of how deeply the Jewish intellectual infection had eaten into the body of our own people. To establish this fact has nothing to do with political denunciations. We are free from any suspicion of wishing to establish petty and irritating regulations for true and genuine art.

**Dr. Goebbels
auf der Jahreskundgebung
der Reichskulturkammer**

Wenn sich die musikalische Jugend in Deutschland zu den atonalen Musikern bekennt, so ist das nur ein Beweis dafür, wie notwendig es ist, rücksichtslos dagegen anzugehen. Wir jedenfalls vermögen weder Vorwärtsweisendes noch Zukunftsträchtiges dabei zu entdecken; wir verwahren uns auf das energischste dagegen, diesen Künstlertypus als deutsch angesprochen zu sehen und buchen die Tatsache seines blutsmäßig rein germanischen Ursprunges nur als praktischen Beweis dafür, wie tief sich die jüdisch-intellektualistische Infizierung bereits in unserem eigenen Volkskörper festgefressen hatte. Das festzulegen, hat nicht das mindeste mit politischem Denunziantentum zu tun. Wir sind erhaben über den Verdacht, wahrer und echter Kunst kleinliche und schikanöse Vorschriften machen zu wollen.

'The foulest perversion of modern music': an extract from Goebbels' denunciation of the (unnamed) Hindemith, December 1934

composer still received an official commission for an orchestral work. He continued to compose as fluently as ever, producing three piano sonatas and another for flute and piano, as well as working on his educational treatise, *Unterweisung im Tonsatz* ('The Craft of Musical Composition'), which contained the fruits of his teaching experience. In the end, the anti-Hindemith lobby had its way: the première by Walter Gieseking in Germany of the first of the piano sonatas was cancelled and his book ended up on display in the 1938 *Entartete Musik* ('Degenerate Music') exhibition, amid all the 'impurities' that had now been purged from German music.

Hindemith began to realize that he was not going to be reconciled with the government of his country. In March 1937, following his third trip to Turkey, he resigned from the Berlin Hochschule. He sailed alone to North America for a short concert tour which included the first overseas performances of the Third Piano Sonata and the Flute Sonata. Appearing as both composer and performer, he played to great acclaim the 1922 Solo Viola Sonata that had so outraged audiences a decade earlier, and was moved to compose and perform another – his Fourth – during the two months he spent there. On his return to Germany in May, he and Gertrud promptly set off for Italy once publication of his book was settled. In Positano they met Stravinsky and his future wife, Vera. Stravinsky's music was

Paul Hindemith mit seiner Frau, einer Tochter des jüdischen Frankfurter Opernkapellmeisters Ludwig Rottenberg, und seinem Verleger.

Paul Hindemith in Baden-Baden.

Eine Erinnerung.

Im Juli 1929 wurde das kommunistische „Lehrstück" von Bert Brecht und Paul Hindemith in Baden-Baden uraufgeführt. Der folgende Bericht über das Werk erschien damals in einer Zeitung im Ruhrgebiet.

„In die Schießbudenatmosphäre eines Jahrmarkts wurde man bei der Aufführung des Fragments „Lehrstück" von Bert Brecht und Paul Hindemith versetzt. Schauplatz dieses Rummels war die Stadthalle, eine ehemalige Turnhalle. An der Decke hängt als Motto ein Plakat mit der Aufschrift: „Besser als Musik hören, ist Musik machen!" Von der Wand hängt ein Flugzeugwrack. Daneben ein Podium, auf dem Orchester und Chor Platz nehmen; an einem Tisch auf dem Podium sitzen Hindemith, Brecht und Gerda Müller, die als Sprecherin fungiert. Auf der Galerie eine Blasmusik aus Lichtenthal, bei deren Gedröhn man nicht weiß, ob sie richtig oder daneben bläst. Dazu ein ausgewähltes Auditorium mit Gerhart Hauptmann, André Gide und sämtlichen badischen Ministern. Das Lehrstück, gegeben durch einige Theorien musikalischer, dramatischer und politischer Art, die auf

Left, 1938 – an attack on Hindemith, the 'Degenerate Musician'. The caption points out Gertrud's Jewish origins: 'Paul Hindemith with his wife, a daughter of the Jewish Frankfurt Opera director Ludwig Rottenberg, and his publisher [Willy Strecker, standing centre]'.

also published by Schott and he had occasionally visited the Hindemiths' flat with Willy Strecker when in Berlin. The two couples distracted themselves from musical matters – Stravinsky was then writing his *Dumbarton Oaks* concerto – by visiting the ruined Roman city of Paestum.

Hindemith's principal reason for this trip to Italy was to meet one of the leading choreographers of the day, Leonide Massine. Various ideas for ballets were proposed; one of them developed into a concert work, the wonderful *Symphonic Dances* for orchestra which were first performed in London in December 1937 and which constitute a second symphony in all but name. Another project – on the life of St Francis of Assisi – reached the stage as the ballet *Nobilissima Visione* and received its first production – again in London – the following summer. The subject may have been suggested by Gertrud, who converted to Roman Catholicism at this time. She and Paul had visited the church of Santa Croce in Florence and been deeply impressed by Giotto's frescoes of the saint. As with *Mathis der Maler*, a concert extract from *Nobilissima Visione* has become one of Hindemith's most successful works; and as with the opera, the ballet's central subject inspired him to write music of a character that belied the stress and insecurity of his situation at home. He also found time to edit the long suppressed Violin Concerto of Robert Schumann, which had been rediscovered by the Hungarian violinist Jelly d'Arányi. Since settling in Berlin, Hindemith's interest in the music of the past had steadily grown, involving him in the arrangement and edition of various works from the Baroque era, by composers such as Johann Sebastian Bach, Heinrich Biber, Karl Stamitz and Antonio Vivaldi.

Following *Nobilissima Visione*, Hindemith turned again to composing sonatas. He decided to write one each with piano accompaniment for all the standard members of the orchestra; only piccolo, double-bassoon and percussion would be excluded. He had written one already for flute and over the next two years completed sonatas for bassoon, oboe (given its première in London the day before *Nobilissima Visione*), viola, violin, clarinet, horn and trumpet, all of which have become staples of the repertoire. In addition, he composed sonatas for piano duet (two pianists at one keyboard) and unaccompanied harp, and several sets of songs. A magnificent and unaccountably neglected Quartet for the unorthodox ensemble of clarinet, violin, cello and piano was first performed in New York on 23 April 1939, during Hindemith's third concert tour of the USA (he had returned to the country in 1938). Yet he still found time to construct a volume of exercises as a sequel to *Unterweisung im Tonsatz*, to compose the Concerto for Violin and Orchestra – which Mengelberg conducted at the première in March 1940 – as well as recompose several songs from *Das Marienleben*, preparing orchestral versions of four of them.

In September 1938, Hindemith finally left Germany and moved to Blusch, a picturesque village in Switzerland. He was reluctant to leave German-speaking Europe altogether, but the *Anschluss* prevented any thoughts of moving to Austria (indeed it precipitated a renewed exodus of Jews and refugees from Nazism) and his international renown made it impossible for him to hide at home for long. A decision was being forced upon him.

Within Hitler's favourite city of Munich, Karl Amadeus Hartmann was able to profit from obscurity. The accession of the Nazi tyranny had coincided with an expansion in scale and maturity in Hartmann's music. He could easily have taken advantage of the vacuum left by the departure of so many composers and secured his own reputation. Instead, he opted for 'internal emigration', withdrawing altogether from German musical life and banning his music from performance inside the German Reich. Thus it was that his first purely orchestral piece, the symphonic poem *Miserae* (1933–4) was

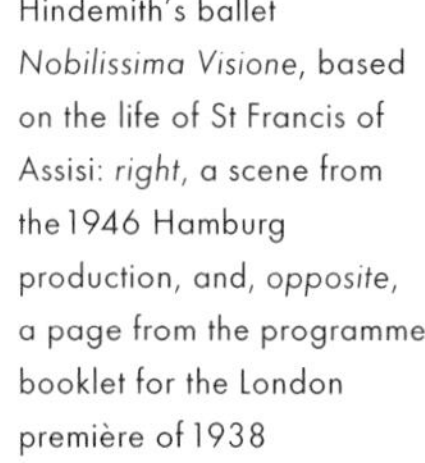

Hindemith's ballet *Nobilissima Visione*, based on the life of St Francis of Assisi: *right*, a scene from the 1946 Hamburg production, and, *opposite*, a page from the programme booklet for the London première of 1938

BALLET RUSSE de MONTE CARLO

WEDNESDAY, JULY 27th, 1938 at 8.45 p.m.

LES ELFES

The ballet excludes a plot and represents in itself a form of pure dance. In this creation Michel Fokine tries to reflect the mood of Mendelssohn's music to the master-piece by Shakespeare. Elves are spirits created by the poetic imagination of peoples of Teutonic or Celtic races. They believe Elves to possess human form, whenever they choose to so present themselves. They then appear in the most beautiful, delicate and airy figures and show themselves fond of music and dancing.

Ballet in One Act by Michel FOKINE
Music of MENDELSSOHN
Choreography by Michel FOKINE
Costumes by Christian BERARD

Mlle. Alicia MARKOVA
M. Igor YOUSKEVITCH

Mlles. Nathalie KRASSOVSKA, CRABOVSKA, MICHAILOVA, GELEZNOVA, RKLITZKA, DROSDOVA, MELNITCHENKO, ROSSON, LAURET, FRANCA, LACCA, LITVINOVA, ETHERIDGE, SCARPOVA, GRANTZEVA, KELEPOVSKA, MLADOVA, KORJINSKA

Mlles. ROUDENKO, POURMEL, FLOTAT, STROGANOVA
MM. Frederic FRANKLIN, Roland GUERARD, GABAY, KIRBOS, FENCHEL, KOKITCH

Orchestra conducted by M. Efrem KURTZ

NOBILISSIMA VISIONE

Young Bernardone gaily spends his days in his father's house at Assisi, devoting his time to the agreeable pastimes in fashion, and surrounded by friends and idlers. Even the little activity he exercises in his father's business is a pleasure to him, as it allows him to meet the buyers who come from all over the world, and his mind, turned towards faraway countries, and his inclination for brave deeds and adventures, constantly find new interests among these people. His youthful pride even causes him to show himself hard-hearted towards the poor; however, it seems that it is following a brutal rebuff on the part of an old beggar that his love of poverty, which will fill all his later life, springs in him; he runs, repenting, after the beggar and gives him part of his riches. Notwithstanding this incident, his taste for chivalrous deeds takes the upper hand. Greatly impressed by the imposing aspect and the superior force of a passing knight who has come to his father's house to replenish his wardrobe, he decides to become a soldier. He girds on weapons, already sees himself, in his imagination, a famous hero, and goes off to war. The severity of a soldier's life, the warrior's cruelty horrify him; finding himself incapable of helping, he becomes desperate.

At that moment, the apparition of three allegorical women shows him that instead of laurels for warriors' deeds, destiny has reserved him a life of quiet piety and self-sacrifice. Apart from chastity and obedience, he will devote himself in particular to poverty. This revelation takes place during a splendid feast, to which he is brought by his friends. They urge him to sing his gay tunes as he did before, and though he does not show himself the boon companion he has once been, they proclaim him king of their burlesque activities. He ought to fall in love, they think, it would do him good. But what can earthly love offer to one who carries in his heart the heavenly vision of Poverty? Remembering her apparition, so full of grace, he distributes plentiful dishes, tablecloths and goblets to the

DL—C

6d.

given its première in Prague, conducted by Hermann Scherchen. Its dedication to 'my friends who had to die a hundred times, who sleep for all eternity; we do not forget you (Dachau 1933–4)' publicly embarrassed the German ambassador. Hartmann wrote later that the advent of the Nazi terror provoked him 'to set down a confession, not of despair or fear of that regime, but of confrontation'. At home, he provoked the authorities as far as he dared. He delayed returning the forms detailing his ethnic origins, required of all government officials and professional persons, until 1936. After the Prague affair an order was imposed on him requiring a fourteen-day notice period in advance of any foreign trips. In due course Hartmann's music was branded 'atonal' and 'degenerate'.

Scherchen was the dedicatee of Hartmann's First String Quartet, written in 1933. Around this time he and Hartmann, aided by Walter Petzet, fashioned a libretto from the sixteenth-century novelist Hans Jakob von Grimmelshausen's epic account of the Thirty Years' War for the opera *Des Simplicius Simplicissimus Jugend*. Hartmann wrote of the impact the book had had on him: 'Its portrayal of the conditions during the Thirty Years' War struck me as extraordinary – "the times are so strange that it's impossible to tell if you'll survive them". This phrase hit me as being relevant today. Once again our people are close to losing their spiritual centre ... There was nothing here that one would expect to find in an opera. It portrays the human race as barbarous, yet I felt that all this was demanding to be put on stage – not as a pleasurable play, but as an urgent message ... To the knowledgeable the *Simplicius* is a reflection of society's fate. It is a judge of today, witness to war and murder.' Hartmann's urgent message was not heard until August 1948, when Hans Rosbaud conducted a concert performance.

Des Simplicius Simplicissimus Jugend contains many allusions to other works, most prominently of all, the Polovtsian Dances from Borodin's *Prince Igor*. Hartmann's opera is a work of considerable power despite the modest forces required (eight solo singers, a chorus and about fifty orchestral players), the vehemence of its ending straining their limitations. This mood was sustained in his next work, a cantata for alto voice and full orchestra, setting poems by the American, Walt Whitman. The thunderous, rampaging drums and granitic brass chords of the first movement are one of Hartmann's

Karl Amadeus Hartmann with his wife Elisabeth in their Munich home, 1939

most immediately memorable inspirations and its elegiac central movements contain some of his deepest and most searching music. The work as a whole did not reach its final, definitive form until 1955. Hartmann even had trouble deciding what to call it, choosing and rejecting *Cantata* and *Lamento* (the latter given in 1937 to a quite separate work for soprano and piano) before settling on *Symphonic Fragments* in 1938. Much revised after the war, Hartmann renamed

Illuſtrierter
Film-Kurier
Erſter Film
von den
Olympiſchen
Spielen
Berlin 1936
882
OLYMPIA
FEST DER VOELKER
Geſtaltung: Leni Riefenſtahl
TONSYSTEM: TOBIS-KLANGFILM

Left, the 'Will to Power': victorious German athleticism portrayed on a film poster for Leni Riefenstahl's *Olympia*, 1936

the work *Versuch eines Requiems* ('Essay Towards a Requiem') and numbered it as his First Symphony.

Hartmann's withdrawal from public view was made economically possible by the personal wealth of Elisabeth, whom he married on 23 December 1934, as soon as she came of age. Fortunately, Reussmann's disapproval did not extend to disinheriting his daughter. Through the Nazi years Elisabeth supported her husband financially. She bore him a son, Richard, on 12 June 1935, their only child.

Much of Hartmann's music of these years would not be performed until well after 1945, and some of it not in his lifetime. The Concerto for Clarinet, String Quartet and String Orchestra, begun in 1930 but not completed until 1935, was one such work. The cantata for soprano, mixed chorus and piano *Friede Anno 48* (1936), setting texts by Andreas Gryphius, had to wait until five years after Hartmann's death before reaching the concert platform, despite being specially commended in Vienna by the jury of the Emil Hertzka Memorial Competition in 1937. An exception was the String Quartet of 1933 with which Hartmann won the 'Carillon' competition in Geneva in 1936. This was Hartmann's first international success, and it received a further performance at the festival of the International Society of Contemporary Music in London in 1938. As Europe drifted towards war, Hartmann began to develop a relationship with Paul Collaer of Belgian Radio. A friend of Scherchen's, Collaer arranged the première of Hartmann's new symphony, based on Emile Zola's novel *L'Oeuvre*, and containing some of his most expressive and virtuoso writing so far. In the same year Hartmann gave vent to his deepening dismay in the beautiful concerto for violin and strings, originally entitled *Musik der Trauer* ('Music of Mourning') but renamed *Concerto funebre* on its revision in 1959. To make his point explicit Hartmann wove into the fabric of this work allusions to hymn tunes of the medieval Czech Hussites – a reference to the betrayal of Czechoslovakia in 1938 – and a Russian revolutionary song later used by Shostakovich in his Eleventh Symphony. The concerto, dedicated to 'my dear son Richard', has a clarity of texture and a classical poise that contrast with the Expressionist tenor of most of Hartmann's music. It was his only work to maintain a toehold, however precarious, in the concert repertoire.

As war approached, the thirteen-year-old Hans Werner Henze was a member of the Hitler Youth. He had come to realize that his father had sold his soul to Hitler, and felt increasingly trapped in a rural backwater. He had also developed a keen interest in music. Encouraged by his mother he began to compose, spurred on after seeing the opera *Le Vin herbé* ('The Drugged Wine') by the Swiss composer, Frank Martin. Martin's music left no lasting mark on Henze but was suggestive of what he could achieve. His father, Franz, was conscripted – not too unwillingly – for the blitzkrieg on Poland. There he was wounded, again in the head, as he had been at Verdun in 1918.

5

A Trail of Unending Misery 1939–45

German civilians evacuating the town of Binsfeld as the US army moves in, 1945

The times were so strange that it was impossible to tell if you'd survive them. The individual was exposed to devastation and the degeneration of an age, in which our nation all but lost its soul. For nowhere was there any deliverance, save in that the spirit of simple folk were able to muster against it.

Hans Jakob von Grimmelshausen,
Simplicius Simplicissimus

A Trail of Unending Misery 1939–45

The war declared on Germany by Great Britain and France on 3 September 1939 did not affect the outcome of Germany's drive to the east. Poland was partitioned between the Nazi and Soviet Russian armies and the West entered a phase of 'phoney war'. Not until April 1940 did German aggression renew itself with the occupation of Denmark and a lightning campaign against Norway, followed a month later by the fall of Holland and Belgium, the disaster at Dunkirk and, on 17 June, the capitulation of the French three days after German troops entered Paris. In little more than two months Hitler had become master of Europe from the Atlantic seaboard to the Soviet border. Within Germany, the Nazis used the pretext of the external conflict to tighten their grip internally, initiating further repression of the minorities they despised. As early as October 1939 Hitler ordered the start of the euthanasia programme, removing mental patients and the handicapped from asylums for execution elsewhere. In late April 1940 enforced deportations of Jews were initiated to officially established ghettos inside Poland.

During the phoney war Hindemith felt in no danger and had to be prised out of Switzerland by friends in Britain and the USA in order to take up part-time lecturing appointments; even then, Gertrud remained behind in Blusch and later experienced difficulties in co-ordinating her escape from Europe when the war was in full swing and shipping in a state of disarray. She did not arrive in New York until mid-September 1940, a full seven months after her husband. He missed the world première of his Violin Concerto in Amsterdam in March but was able to hear the piece when the conductor Sergey Koussevitsky included it in the programmes of the Boston Symphony Orchestra. At the end of April 1940, following some lectures, he was offered a post as visiting professor of music theory at Yale University to commence in September. Through the summer Hindemith ran a workshop at Koussevitsky's instigation at the Berkshire Music Festival summer school at Tanglewood. Three of his students there went on to achieve international prominence as composers in their own right: the young German emigré, Lukas Foss, Harold Shapero, and, best known of all, Leonard Bernstein. Towards the end of the festival, in which several compositions of his – including the *Mathis der Maler* symphony – were featured, Hindemith's Third Sonata for Organ (composed early that year and, as with *Der Schwanendreher*, based on old folk-songs) received its première. Five weeks later in Boston, Lukas Foss was the solo pianist in a concert performance of Hindemith's ballet, *The Four Temperaments*. The music, scored for piano and string orchestra, originated in a project devised by Massine for a ballet inspired by paintings of the fifteenth-century Flemish artist, Brueghel. As with an earlier idea based on the work of the Italian, Fra Angelico, the Brueghel project fell through and composer and choreographer became estranged. However, in collaboration with another eminent dancer of Russian origin, George Balanchine, Hindemith adapted the music to a new scenario based on the ancient idea of the four temperaments that in combination make up the human psyche, an inspiration that several other composers have followed before and since, not least Carl Nielsen and Robert Simpson. Hindemith's sequence of the melancholic–sanguine–phlegmatic–choleric is unusual but was designed to fit in with a formal scheme where each temperament had its own movement. These in turn are variations on an opening 'theme', itself a five-minute movement built out of three themes heard at the outset.

In addition to the ballet, the ever-productive composer completed two major orchestral works in his first year of North American exile: the exhilarating Symphony in E flat and his third Concerto for Cello and Orchestra. All three have proved with time to rank amongst his finest music, although their entry into public awareness was not as rapid as Hindemith had been used to. After its concert performance, *The Four Temperaments* was not staged until 1946, and then for a single night only. The concerto was first performed by the leading cellist, Gregor Piatigorsky, in Boston on 7 February 1941. The symphony had to wait until 21 November when Dimitri Mitropoulos conducted it in Minneapolis. It is a bracing, optimistic work, extrovert and invigorating in character, not unlike a fifth *Konzertmusik* writ large for a full orchestra. Yet there are also, especially in the slow

second movement, moments of rather darker inspiration where the sense of relief – as if of escape from some implicit terror – is manifest.

After the bold statements of ballet, concerto and symphony, in 1941 and 1942 Hindemith set his sights rather lower. His teaching commitments at Yale demanded a considerable amount of time and he concentrated on extending his series of sonatas, adding ones for cor anglais, trombone and a 'little' sonata for cello. Two important musical works appeared in 1942: the lively Sonata for Two Pianos (which shares with the 1939 Harp Sonata the formal conceit of constructing an entire movement as an unsung setting of a poem, something which Henze contrived in the finale of his Seventh Symphony four decades later) and *Ludus tonalis*, an hour-long sequence of fugues and interludes, with framing prelude and postlude, for solo piano and styled 'studies in counterpoint, tonal organization and piano playing'. Whatever didactic purpose lay behind the various tricks of its construction (the closing postlude is a palindrome of the opening prelude), *Ludus tonalis* is an astonishing display of compositional skill: it is far and away his finest work for the piano (and the largest), occupying a position in his output not unlike that of *The Art of Fugue* to Johann Sebastian Bach's or the *Fantasia contrappuntistica* to that of Busoni. In the following year, Hindemith completed his third book, *A Concentrated Course in Traditional Harmony*, again placing the experience of his tuition – this time at Yale – on permanent record.

Left, the victorious German army unfurl the Swastika over conquered Paris, June 1940

Even before Hitler's armies achieved their greatest victories surging far into Russia after breaking the Nazi–Soviet pact in 1941, Karl Amadeus Hartmann in Munich had reflected that war was 'the greatest of all the crimes of tyranny' and composed a *Sinfonia tragica*. In two slow, sombre movements, Hartmann constructed a powerfully eloquent lament for the continent that was being ripped apart. He was not writing from the splendid isolation of an ivory tower. The tyrannical regime that he hated was an ever-oppressive presence around him.

The *Sinfonia tragica* was dedicated to Paul Collaer, who had planned to give the opera, *Des Simplicius Simplicissimus Jugend*, its première at the end of May 1940, before the German occupation of Belgium prevented its realization. Collaer was also unable to perform the *Sinfonia tragica*, but did ensure its rehearsal before returning the score to Hartmann, together with some suggested alterations.

Following page, one of many trails of unending misery as Jews endure enforced deportation in Würzburg, 1942

A scene from the first production of Hindemith's ballet *The Four Temperaments*, by the New York City Ballet, 1946

Hartmann's personal conduct during the Nazi period as a whole is shrouded in mystery. His stance of internal emigration was a courageous act for a man with a young wife and family, but at no time was he inclined to abandon Nazified Munich. 'I could never leave this city. She holds tightly to those who have made their names in her, even when she does not seem very accommodating,' he wrote. There have been suggestions of greater involvement in opposition to the Nazis. Hans Moldenhauer, in his biography of Anton von Webern (1978), states in a footnote that at 'a time when the tidal wave of political nationalism swept his native country, Karl Amadeus Hartmann was one of the first to profess a pacifist creed and to engage in underground resistance against the Hitler regime'. Moldenhauer was a friend of Hartmann's and was the dedicatee of the composer's final, unfinished work, *Gesangsszene*. Later in his book Moldenhauer goes further: 'Hartmann was a man of buoyant temperament and great charm. Politically, he belonged to a small group of Germans who, from the beginning, had adamantly opposed the Hitler regime. He escaped military service by going into hiding for long periods of time, and with a few trusted friends he formed the nucleus of a resistance movement.' Many Germans were executed for less, yet nowhere are these friends and activities recorded. In the post-Nazi period, such conduct should have elevated him to hero status. Yet Hartmann himself never advertised it, nor do his autobiographical writings make reference to any underground activity. In the paranoia of post-war Germany, the Western powers retained much of the Nazi administrative apparatus intact, especially in Bavaria. This might explain a later reticence on Hartmann's part but his widow is categoric in her denial of any involvement by any member of the Hartmann family in underground resistance.

One possible explanation for this disparity may lie in several circumstantial facts that in isolation amount to little but when taken together could be construed as significant. Karl's brother Richard had distributed leaflets against Hitler during the presidential campaign in 1932. On Hitler's assumption of the chancellorship the following year he fled to Switzerland, where he remained until 1946. Karl himself never belonged to any political party, though his Socialist sympathies were not unknown. He was summoned on several occasions to attend medical examinations to determine his fitness for military service. Judicious use of tablets causing profuse perspiration was sufficient for a final verdict to be deferred until a local art-loving medical director confirmed and certificated Hartmann's unfitness for duty. Hartmann managed to help a pianist friend, Martin Piper, to dodge the draft at another examination by administering a disgusting concoction of

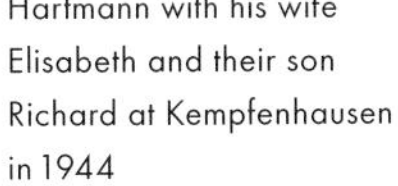

Hartmann with his wife Elisabeth and their son Richard at Kempfenhausen in 1944

Hindemith at Yale demonstrating his proficiency – which extended to an enormous variety of instruments – on the trumpet, with wife Gertrud accompanying him on the piano 'boiled washing soap, cigars and cognac'. Small beer perhaps, but enough to cost him liberty, or life, if he had been caught. His bravery and dissidence were never in doubt.

Hartmann's decision to cut himself off from musical life in Germany was definitely an act of conscience and one that he sustained more consistently than any German artist. Cut off by his own decision from the mainstream, he went to study in 1942 with the semi-outlawed Anton von Webern, the former pupil and associate of Arnold Schoenberg and promulgator of Schoenberg's revolutionary twelve-note method, which systematized atonality by use of the twelve notes within the octave arranged in rigid series. Schoenberg had fled to the United States in 1934 following the Nazi accession to power, followed in 1938 by his students and colleagues in Austria. This left Webern, a minor aristocrat and racially 'pure', as the sole remaining exponent of Viennese radicalism. The roots of this tradition lay ultimately in the music of Mahler, which as Hartmann noted in a letter to his wife, 'Webern praised at every available opportunity'. As a matter of course Mahler's Jewish origins had rendered his music unacceptable to the Nazis. Webern had far outstripped Schoenberg in his extreme application of 'serial' techniques to rhythm and instrumentation as well as melody and harmony. Webern's music had been labelled as degenerate and banned, despite his strongly pro-right political affinities. If he was viewed as something of a totem by Hartmann it was for musical rather than political or 'confrontational' reasons.

Hartmann first consulted Webern – in 1941 – by letter, asking whether Universal Edition in Vienna, who were Webern's publishers, might take on his music. Nothing came of this, but Hartmann was sufficiently encouraged to travel to Maria-Enzersdorf near Vienna, where Webern lived, in order to study with him. Hartmann learned to be careful and keep his political differences with Webern apart from his musical studies, as well as separate from his respect and admiration for the man. In the same letter to his wife, Hartmann wrote, 'I was largely to blame that the conversation repeatedly turned to politics. This was a mistake, because with my strong sympathies towards anarchism I discovered things that I would have preferred not to. The main thing was that he seriously held the view that all authority should be respected for the sake of good order, and that one should – no matter what the price – recognize the State in which one lives.'

Hartmann was of a very different cast as a composer and he learned much from Webern's method, without adopting his methodology. Little of Webern's direct influence is discernible in Hartmann's later music, except perhaps negatively in the general avoidance of serial techniques. A few works, such as the Fourth Symphony (1948), do make use of themes with twelve-note properties, but Hartmann always remained at heart a composer working within traditional means, however freely interpreted. He recognized the nature of his debt to Webern in a later letter to his wife: 'In the end you could say that not only did I learn a great deal about composing from Webern, but that due to him I also became a more orderly person.' The tuition he received was in the form of extended analyses covering a wide range of music, including Beethoven piano sonatas, Reger string quartets and Webern's own Variations for Piano of 1935–6. One particularly memorable session included an off-the-cuff exposition on Schoenberg's early opera, *Erwartung* ('Expectation'). Some of Hartmann's own scores were gone through, including *Des Simplicius Simplicissimus Jugend* and what he termed 'my first symphony'. It is unclear which symphony this might be: *Versuch eines Requiems* would not be called a symphony for eight more years, so either the 1938 Symphony for string orchestra and soprano or that based on Zola's *L'Oeuvre* could be meant. It is even possible that the work referred to is the *Sinfonia tragica*. Pupil and teacher did not always concur in their opinions of other composers' stature. 'Even as I heartily rejoice at his opinion of Reger I cannot agree with his appraisal of Bruckner. He does not believe that Bruckner has contributed to the development of music. Is Bruckner then so different from Mahler?' This remark encapsulates the essential difference between pupil and teacher. Webern's music sprang ultimately from a Mahlerian, high-romantic aesthetic, whereas Hartmann was preternaturally Brucknerian in orientation. The music of Anton Bruckner also linked Hartmann to Hindemith in spirit. The Icelandic composer Jon Thórarinsson who studied at Yale between 1944 and 1947 recalled that, among 'the composers of the Classic and Romantic period, Anton Bruckner was the one most often referred to by Hindemith.

I believe he considered Bruckner, who at this time was practically unknown in America, to be the greatest symphonist after Beethoven.'

The period of study with Webern occurred during the composition of one of Hartmann's largest projects up to that time, *Sinfoniae dramaticae*. It comprises a symphonic overture, originally entitled *China kämpft* ('China's Struggle'), three symphonic hymns and a suite for orchestra with reciter, *Vita nova* ('New Life'). The entire set was completed in 1943 and Hartmann then turned to revising the *Sinfonia tragica* by incorporating Collaer's suggested alterations into the first movement. He worried over the safety of his manuscripts as aerial bombardments were increasing in intensity and the prospect of invasion seemed now the only outcome to end the war. Accordingly, Hartmann collected the most valuable of his manuscripts, including the opera, string quartet and the recent large symphonic pieces and 'placed my works in a case which was soldered and buried two metres deep in a mountain'. In 1944, the arrest of a close friend, Robert Havemann, prompted Hartmann into commencing a new symphony – his fourth – entitled *Klagegesang* ('Hymn of Lamentation'). He subsequently subtitled the work 'symphonic expressions' as if unsure of its credentials as a symphony. Even more than with the *Symphonic Fragments*, *Klagegesang* caused Hartmann considerable difficulty to get right. The initial version appears to have been substantively complete by the following year, but Hartmann continued to work at it until 1947. Concurrently with the work on *Klagegesang*, Hartmann began to evolve another symphonic work, the *Adagio* for large orchestra which eventually became the second of his numbered symphonies. The roots of the *Adagio* lay in the *Vita nova* Suite; whether his re-use of some of the material was occasioned by dissatisfaction with the earlier work can now only be guessed at.

Vita nova was lost (and part of it remains so), while the *Sinfonia tragica* was to disappear for over forty years en route to Belgium when Hartmann despatched it in 1946 to Collaer for the much-delayed première. In both works and life, wartime cast a shadow over Hartmann that took years to dispel.

Hindemith's new works were premièred fairly quickly by top rank conductors such as Koussevitsky, Eugene Ormandy and Artur Rodzinki. The orchestral *Symphonic Metamorphoses on Themes by*

Carl Maria von Weber, first performed by the New York Philharmonic, was salvaged by Hindemith from yet another abortive ballet project with Massine. The music betrays nothing of its balletic origins and is as spontaneous and exuberant a work as the title is clumsy. Here, more than in his orchestral concertos, Hindemith produced a virtuoso showpiece to rival Bartók's famous concerto of 1943. It has proved to be one of his most-played orchestral works. The ballet *Hérodiade*, after a poem by Mallarmé, has remained almost completely unknown. Hindemith composed it for the great American dancer and choreographer Martha Graham, who created the title role in its première on 30 October 1944. The music of *Hérodiade* has a calm and elusive character, a development from *The Four Temperaments* rather than a continuation of the *Symphonic Metamorphoses.*

The unwilling soldier: a passport photograph of the eighteen-year-old Hans Werner Henze in uniform, 1944–5.

The young Hans Werner Henze increased his musical activity considerably during the early years of the war, to the detriment of his schoolwork. He was 'sinking all the time in my production of Latin, mathematics, *et cetera*, because I was completely taken by music. I practised [the piano], I composed. There was a chamber music group that would meet twice a week and I wrote pieces for them to play ... but I just could not make myself do anything for my school any more. So it was decided that I should go and study music.' Some of his early efforts came to the attention of Wilhelm Maler, a professor of music in Cologne, who 'gave me enormous encouragement'. A student of Maler's living in a neighbouring village showed Henze scores of forbidden works by Mahler and Hindemith, as well as by some of the younger generation. She also lent him a book on the history of music which had a large section on contemporary composers, with colour likenesses of Stravinsky, Berg and Schoenberg.

Henze was despatched in 1941 to an academy in Braunschweig, where an aunt was asked to keep an eye on him. There Henze learned not just about music but of the course of the war. 'There were teachers who came back missing an arm or a leg and they would tell you the most terrible stories about what the Germans did in Poland. I also knew there were concentration camps and what happened in them.' In an autobiographical article written some four decades later, Henze reflected on Germans who claimed to have known nothing:

The tide turns in the West as the Allies invade Normandy, 6 June 1944.

If someone like myself, a fifteen-year-old living in the depths of the country, knew about the concentration camps by the beginning of the 1940s, then other people, the adults, definitely knew better than me what was going on. A neighbour's fiancé in our village, Senne II near Bielefeld – and this is just one example – was in the SS and sometimes came home on leave. His bride told me at the wedding reception that her handsome, tall, proud, Jürgen had terrible nightmares, ever since he had begun to serve in a concentration camp and had to do guard duty at night on the watchtowers. From there he could see how the prisoners would deliberately kill themselves by clambering on the electrified barbed-wire. He couldn't bear to watch it any more. He was hoping for a transfer. While Jürgen's bride was telling me this I could hear my father, in his Nazi uniform, roaming drunkenly through the woods with his party cronies, bawling out repulsive songs: 'When Jewish blood splashes off your knife'. These are traumatic memories.

Following page, 'Twilight of the Gods': the Hammer and Sickle flies over the Reichstag as the Red Army takes Berlin, April 1945

Henze did not have long to enjoy his freedom at Braunschweig. In January 1944 he was drafted, and in late March assigned to an armoured division stationed near Magdeburg. He was trained as a signaller and was able secretly to listen in to foreign broadcasts of news or music, both of which were strictly forbidden. His entire company learned of the Normandy invasions on 6 June 1944 and

Anti-tank defences in Germany, erected in a vain effort to keep the Allies at bay

With the Reich in ruins, German civilians pick their way over rubble to the safety of Allied occupied territory in Dresden, 1945

Henze and a friend celebrated with a bottle of wine. They saw action that year against the Russians, mainly in Hungary, though he was not directly involved in fighting. As Henze recalls: 'Thank God I was never in a tank, nor in a tank battle.' The German army suffered appalling losses in a whole series of engagements against the Russian armoured divisions in Hungary; of Henze's company only five survived. The proto-Fascist Hungarian government capitulated to the Russians and then turned their guns on their erstwhile German allies. Henze was transferred to Denmark where he remained until the surrender in May 1945. He was then marched with the rest of the occupation force back to Germany, fetching up in Schleswig-Holstein, within the British zone. The defeated troops were herded across a river on to a small peninsula. 'The British army simply occupied the river and what was inside was the responsibility of the German army still, including the feeding of these crowds of prisoners ... food was very scarce indeed.'

The march of another line of prisoners had been witnessed hundreds of miles to the south near Munich by Hartmann a few days earlier, during the night of 27–28 April 1945. These prisoners – 20,000 of them – were being transported from Dachau. A Gauleiter

'Endless the stream ... endless the misery ... endless the sorrow': , the enforced transportation of prisoners from the concentration camp at Dachau prompted the composition of Hartmann's Piano Sonata '27 April 1945'. Within days, as pictured here, the inmates were liberated by US troops.

who lived across the street from Hartmann caused pandemonium when his staff distributed bread to the prisoners, who were on the edge of starvation. The sight profoundly moved Hartmann and directly provoked the composition of his Piano Sonata '27 April 1945'. The inscription on the score records the doleful inspiration: 'endless was the stream – endless the misery – endless the sorrow'. This was Hartmann's second sonata, but it did not escape the composer's growing self-criticism. Dissatisfied with the fourth and final movement he provided a condensed alternative version. Even then, the sonata did not receive its première until June 1982. In the immediate aftermath of the German collapse – with the revelations of the Germans' systematic extermination of half of Europe's Jews, as well as other smaller ethnic groups including Slavs and gypsies – music and its performance seemed almost impossible to countenance.

Ruin and Resurgence 1945–53

6

Women move masonry from the shell of the Hofkirche, Dresden, 1945

The days in Germany are wonderful. To you of course it seems odd that contact with one's old home can be so lovely in spite of all the misery. But an afternoon like that at your house, with the Krapfen *and the cosy coffee table, is something that through all these years one has been pining for.*

Gertrud Hindemith,
letter to Ludwig Strecker, 1949

Ruin and Resurgence 1945–53

Opposite, bombed-out central Cologne, in 1945 – a panorama of desolation

Elsewhere, music recovered remarkably quickly, as a German tourist brochure, *The Muses on the Banks of the Spree*, recorded. 'After the New Apocalypse, very few members were still in possession of their instruments. Hardly a musician could call a decent suit his own. Yet, by the early summer of 1945, strains of sweet music floated on the air again. While the town still reeked of smoke, charred buildings and the stench of corpses, the [Berlin] Philharmonic Orchestra bestowed the everlasting and imperishable joy which music never fails to give.' Whether or not, as the poet D. J. Enright wrote in response to this passage, 'one Bach outweighs ten Belsens', music's power to heal became a political symbol of the resurrection of national culture for both conquerors and conquered. It also provoked less worthy sentiments. Henze observed of an audience after a performance of the *Mathis der Maler* symphony in Bielefeld: 'There was an undertone of "Now that Hindemith can be played again, our guilt is removed, everything is right with the world again, isn't it?"'

Germany in 1945 was not permitted to put its own house in order as it had attempted to do by revolution in 1918. The country was carved up between the four principal victorious powers. Britain took the northwestern segment, Russia the east (after ceding a large tract of German territory, including Silesia, to its reconstituted vassal state of Poland), the USA the south and France the mid-west. As at the end of the Great War, an uprising in Bavaria against the defeated government failed, not least from inopportune timing. Suppressed on the day of its inception (28 April, when the trail of prisoners had trudged past the Hartmann home), the rebellion anticipated by just forty-eight hours Hitler's suicide in the Berlin bunker. While the new Führer, Grand Admiral Karl von Dönitz, exhorted the people to fight on, much of the Nazi hierarchy attempted either to escape or kill themselves. The unconditional surrender on 7 May left a provisional government functioning under Dönitz until 23 May when it was

Following page, slowly, the rebuilding begins as women start to clear bomb damage in Berlin, 1945

formally dissolved and the Allied powers took over the running of the divided country.

Even as the Allied armies were crossing the Rhine in the west and the Oder in the east, diplomatic battle-lines were already drawn in full for a new conflict between the capitalist Western powers and the Soviet Union. Henze became aware of the shifts in alignment while still a prisoner-of-war in Schleswig-Holstein. 'It went so far that in my camp there were many people who were almost convinced that we would change uniforms and march against the Russians with the British and the French and the Americans as allies. But that was the general feeling – many thought it could happen.'

Hard-line and top-ranking Nazis may have been put on trial, excluded from high office and subjected to de-Nazification, but the paranoia of both sides led them to recruit the lower echelons. Opponents of Hitler's regime were placed at times in positions of authority, but much of the day-to-day work continued to be performed by former party sympathizers. Hence, Hartmann was appointed with the approval of the American administration to oversee the revitalization of musical culture in Bavaria, centred on the State Opera in Munich. Hartmann was almost the sole prominent musical figure in the American zone wholly untainted by either Fascist or Communist sympathies. He conceived of a new concert series which would act as a blueprint for the rest of the country: Musica Viva. In this series Hartmann promoted music that had been written or banned during the years of the Third Reich, introducing German audiences to all they had missed. He also vigorously pursued young composers and young listeners. Up to 200 seats were withheld until the day of performance when they were made available at reduced prices for students.

New concert initiatives were developed elsewhere in Germany, often with a special emphasis on modern music. The partition of the country into four zones encouraged a regional rather than national approach to music-making, a policy that persisted after the amalgamation in 1949 of the British, French and American territories. ('Trizonia', as it was known, was the direct precursor of the Federal Republic of Germany which was formally established on 21 September that year.) One of the earliest and most progressive of these institutions was Southwest German Radio, based in Baden-Baden.

This operated under initial French patronage and made a speciality of music composed after 1933. The most influential new music establishment became the annual composers' summer school held at Darmstadt under the auspices of the Kranichsteiner Music Institute. One of the highlights of the first rough-and-ready affair (which actually took place in the autumn of 1946) was a performance of Hindemith's *Lehrstück* in its entirety, conducted by Henze, who recalls 'There was a great deal of discussion about the text and its meaning, but nobody discussed Hindemith's music.' Henze, aged twenty, secured a notable success at Darmstadt that year with the première on 27 September of his Chamber Concerto for piano, flute and strings. Willy Strecker from Schott was present and immediately offered Henze a publishing contract. The three H's – Hindemith, Hartmann, Henze – came with the same colophon, and a continuity of sorts was created for the central core of German creativity. Schott remain to this day the major publisher of mainstream German modernism.

In succeeding years the Darmstadt summer school attracted progressives from an increasingly international field, in the process evolving a Vatican-like attitude of avant-garde infallibility. Many composers, Henze included, found this unacceptable, but in the first years extreme prejudices were kept at bay and all styles mixed. In 1947 the French composer, René Leibowitz, a pupil of both Schoenberg and Webern, began to teach analysis of Schoenberg's music, a development of incalculable importance for the future of European composition as a whole. That same year Hartmann's overture *China kämpft* was given its première, making a considerable impression.

Away from the exalted atmosphere of summer school and festival, the painstaking day-to-day exhumation of Germany's musical culture continued, not least in the field of education. Following his release by the British and demobilization in August 1945, Henze was anxious to resume his musical studies. Various possibilities were advanced, including a move to Berlin for tuition with the composer Boris Blacher. This involved crossing illegally from the British into first the American then the French zones for an audition at Tübingen. Such movements required visas which were next-to-impossible to obtain, so Henze crawled by night across railway lines and proceeded by stealth into the French zone. He was arrested and spent a week doing hard labour in a makeshift camp before being deported. At length, Henze managed to secure a place at the Institute of Evangelical Church Music at Heidelberg, studying composition with Wolfgang Fortner. Fortner was a distinguished composer who had continued to teach at the Institute throughout the Nazi period, although his compositions did not always enjoy official favour. Fortner specialized in the music of Johann Sebastian Bach. 'A very good education for a composer,' Henze recalls, 'counterpoint, the old keys'. To pay his way, Henze was engaged as a live-in tutor to the three children of a local law professor, Dr Adolf Schüle, and remained there until his graduation in the summer of 1948.

Henze's early compositions reflect the combination of craftsmanship instilled at Heidelberg with the shock of the new learned at Darmstadt. Stravinsky, Hindemith, Bartók are much in evidence as models. The music of the Second Viennese School took longer to assimilate. Henze never adopted serial procedures into his music wholeheartedly, but was keen to try his hand at anything. In 1947 he composed his First Symphony, the slow movement of which was performed at Darmstadt under Scherchen's baton. Fortner premièred the entire four-movement work the following year. (In 1963 Henze thoroughly recomposed the work as a chamber symphony, removing one movement altogether.) Music poured from his pen in 1949 and 1950, including a short opera (*Das Wundertheater* – 'The Magic Theatre'), two more symphonies, concertos for piano and for violin, two sets of variations and three ballet scores.

His interest in ballet was kindled in 1948 when he was invited to Hamburg to watch the visiting Sadler's Wells ballet company. 'It was like a revelation of the first order. I didn't know that kind of dance existed. Marvellous, really marvellous, a week of a new theatrical art.' Henze began working as the musical director of a theatre company in Constance that same year and in 1950 moved to Wiesbaden to direct the ballet of the Hesse State Theatre. Despite much tiresome arranging of other composers' ballet music and constant rehearsing, Henze was able to compose the *Ballet Variations, Jack Pudding* and *Rosa Silber*. The buoyant and vivacious Third Symphony, completed in the same year as these ballets, shares their dance-like character and internal structure. It is a symphony in name only.

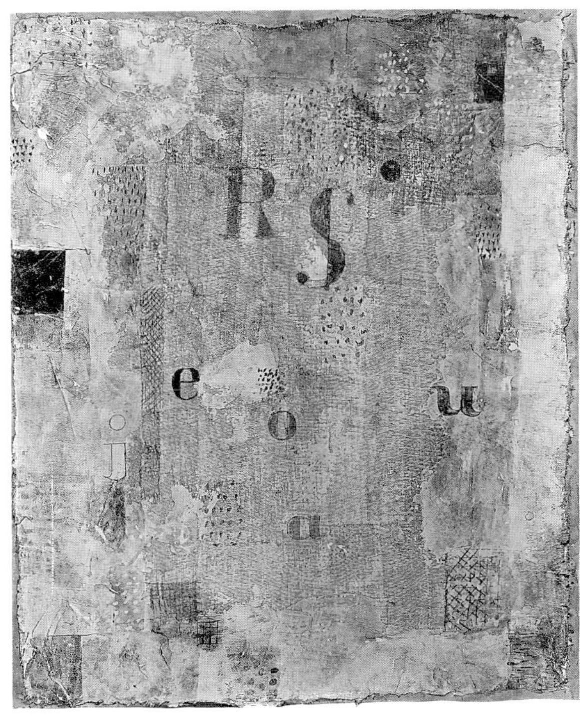

Above, Paul Klee's painting *Vocal Fabric of the Singer Rosa Silber*, 1922, which shares its inspiration with that of Henze's third ballet
Left, Henze at the piano with Professor Dr Hans Hoffmann in 1949

Henze, until his appointment at Wiesbaden, was under intense personal and financial stress. He had begun to feel acutely aware of what he later termed his 'social isolation' as a homosexual, with its threat of imprisonment and public disgrace. In the winter of 1948 he and his Italian lover were arrested in a dawn raid following a complaint from his landlady and subjected to lengthy police questioning. In early 1950 Henze moved to West Berlin but ran into serious debt and became ill. The composer Paul Dessau, who had returned to East Berlin in 1948, visited Henze in hospital and became a good friend. Dessau's Marxist convictions evoked a sympathetic response in the younger composer: 'I owe a great deal of my political education to him, a Marxist and humanistic moralist.' It was Dr Schüle from Heidelberg who extricated Henze from Berlin, invited him to stay the summer and helped him secure the position with the Hesse State Theatre.

Down in Munich, Hartmann's compositional activity was constrained by his Musica Viva duties and by a dissatisfaction with much of his earlier music. During 1947–53 he proceeded to reconstruct his entire symphonic output. Of the early proto-symphonies dating from 1932, to *Klagegesang* in 1947, only *Miserae* (1933–4) remained untouched. *Symphonic Fragments*, revised in 1954–5, was recast as his 'Symphony No. 1'. The *Adagio* for large orchestra completed during the war was designated No. 2. During 1948–9, Hartmann cannibalized the unperformed *Klagegesang*, adding to it the opening movement of the *Sinfonia tragica* to form the Third Symphony. The full score of the *Sinfonia tragica* had been lost in transit to Belgium and did not resurface until the 1970s in the archives of Belgian Radio. The dolorous inspiration of both of the earlier works was encapsulated more convincingly in the new symphony than before, its atmosphere of tragedy more compellingly achieved. Hartmann also no longer felt the need to retain an affirmative close. The Third Symphony, conducted by Erich Schmid at its première in February 1950, ranks as one of Hartmann's most accomplished works.

The Second Symphony, the single-movement *Adagio*, was conducted seven months later, at Donaueschingen by Hans Rosbaud. Its success provided a model for Hartmann to follow in salvaging the unused music of *Klagegesang* as a self-contained symphonic

Left, the Master Craftsman of musical composition: Hindemith at Yale, late 1940s

Thórarinsson and his wife, Edda Kvaran, enjoyed a closer relationship with his teacher than did most of the students, perhaps because of their common European heritage. That the childless Paul and Gertrud Hindemith felt real affection for the Icelander is attested by their fondness for his son, Thórarinn. On one occasion, at the end of the school day:

Only the two of us [Hindemith and Thórarinsson] remained in the classroom, when my wife appeared with our little boy. Hindemith immediately forgot everything else, started playing with the little one, crawling under the piano, pretending to be a dog or a bear, and putting on all kinds of funny acts until the boy, a little scared at first, became absolutely absorbed in the game. I do not think that many people ever saw this very tender and humane side of the great man's personality. In the spring my boy received from the Hindemiths the largest Easter bunny I have ever seen.

The work at Yale took its toll on Hindemith's compositional output. Apart from his setting of the Walt Whitman poem only the *Symphonia serena*, commissioned by the Dallas Symphony Orchestra, was completed in 1946 (with some of his students writing out the orchestral parts). The next year saw the motet *Apparebit repentina dies*, and a Clarinet Concerto for the great jazz performer, Benny Goodman. In 1948 he produced his third and last Sonata for Cello and Piano and the fine Septet for Wind Instruments. The major event of that year was the much-delayed release of his new version of the song-cycle *Das Marienleben*. This had been complete since before the end of the war, but Hindemith was unusually sensitive to the work's reception. He prefaced the score with a defence of his revisions, which prompted considerable debate for many years. The two versions can be seen now as distinct views, equal in worth, of the same material from different points in the composer's career.

Hindemith and his wife decided to make visits to Europe from 1947 as part of concert tours which did not always include engagements in Germany. Their attempt to visit Frankfurt quietly in May 1947 was discovered. It obliged them to attend performances of some older works of his that Paul would rather have avoided. Such revivals became a feature of subsequent tours and thus he remade his acquaintance with *Cardillac, Neues vom Tage* and *Mathis der Maler*, all of which proved to be distractions from the formulation of a new large-scale opera to be based on the life of the late medieval astronomer, Johannes Kepler. A production in Venice of *Cardillac* spurred Hindemith to rewrite completely this early opera. He replaced Ferdinand Lion's original libretto with one of his own and interjected a new and largely superfluous third act. He then forbade performances of the original version, a case of the creator not so much killing the owner of his art as in the opera, but destroying the art itself. Since Hindemith's death the second version of *Cardillac*, with which he continued to tinker at times throughout the 1950s, has been eclipsed by its predecessor. In 1953, Hindemith turned to *Cardillac*'s successor, *Neues vom Tage*. Although the changes effected were on a much less drastic scale, he again replaced the libretto with one of his own and had to be persuaded only with great difficulty from excising the infamous bathroom scene that had caused him so much trouble.

Hindemith in 1949 composed three concertos for wind instruments, one for the outstanding British horn virtuoso Dennis Brain. The Sonata for Double Bass and Piano revived Hindemith's sonata series, but aside from his operatic revisions, the main thrust of his output in the early 1950s was concentrated in two unremarkable symphonic works and a third, based on projected music for the Kepler opera, now titled *Die Harmonie der Welt* ('The Harmony of the World'). Like the symphony from *Mathis der Maler*, that from *Die Harmonie der Welt* forms a triptych evoking three poetic ideas of the parent opera's hero. The movements depict in turn 'musica instrumentalis', that played by instruments or voices, 'musica humana', formed by the interplay of two souls in love, and 'musica mundana', the music of the spheres. Commissioned by Hindemith's Swiss supporter Paul Sacher, the symphony *Die Harmonie der Welt* was conducted by its dedicatee in Basel on 25 January 1952.

Hindemith's sixth and final book, *A Composer's World*, published in 1952, derived from a series of six lectures given in late 1949 at Harvard University. The presentation of these lectures was a signal honour and Hindemith took his commitment seriously enough to take a year off from Yale to prepare them. He even missed his mother's funeral in November 1949 to avoid cancelling the final lecture. *A Composer's World* is unique amongst Hindemith's books

Opposite, the title page of Hindemith's opera *The Harmony of the World*, based on the life of the astronomer Johannes Kepler and begun as a symphony in 1951

PAUL
HINDEMITH
DIE HARMONIE
DER WELT
EDITION SCHOTT
4925

in that it is neither a technical manual nor a textbook, but an extended discussion of musical aesthetics, of the meaning of music rather than its means.

His leave of absence from Yale in 1949–50 marked a turning-point in Hindemith's relationship to America just as, for very different reasons, the enforced leave from the Berlin Hochschule in 1934–5 had clarified his views about Germany. When he resumed teaching at Yale in November 1950 it was on a changed basis of year-on, year-off, the periods away being devoted to his new professorial post at the university in Zurich, Switzerland. This arrangement did not last; Hindemith was anxious to get to grips with his Kepler opera and to fulfil a commission from UNESCO (United Nations Educational, Scientific and Cultural Organisation) for a three-part oratorio using a text by the French writer, Paul Claudel. Something had to give, and it proved to be his commitment to Yale. The lure of Europe, made

A scene from the première in Munich of *The Harmony of the World*, finally completed in 1957

more enticing by the glimpses seen during the post-war tours, was irresistible. Since Hindemith felt he could not return to Germany to live, Zurich became his new home from June 1953.

By a curious quirk of fate, as the Hindemiths were preparing for their return in early 1953, Henze emigrated from Germany. His sense of alienation had gathered pace for a variety of reasons. His isolation as a homosexual in an aggressive, intolerant, heterosexual society carried personal risk. His left-wing politics and deep-seated shame over the Holocaust made it increasingly difficult for him to accept the authority of so many former Nazi officials, exacerbated by the intensifying cold war raging over Germany between the American and Soviet governments. And finally there was Italy. He had visited the country on holiday in 1951 and was amazed. 'I had no idea that buildings, towns, landscapes could be so movingly beautiful. To see unbombed cities – whenever I saw a city in Germany I saw its shell, or it had been razed to the ground.' Henze felt close politically and culturally to the Italians. 'These people had resisted the Nazis ... they were heroes who had fought Fascism, working class. So I felt I must do everything to go to Italy.' Henze's contractual obligations as director at Wiesbaden delayed the move and in the ensuing year he was kept busy enough with his compositions. The first performance of his Third Symphony took place in Donaueschingen conducted by Rosbaud on 7 October, and six weeks later his single-act radio opera *Ein Landarzt* ('A Country Doctor', after Franz Kafka's short story) was broadcast from Hamburg. On 17 February 1952, Henze's first full-length opera, *Boulevard Solitude*, based on the story of Manon Lescaut, was staged in Hanover to a packed house. This production brought Henze to the notice of a wider audience than any of his contemporaries. Further premières included two more ballets, *Labyrinth* and *Der Idiot* (the latter after Dostoevsky's novel). This sustained exposure opened a rift, minor at first, between Henze and the other young lions, principally Stockhausen and Boulez, who congregated annually at Darmstadt. While Adorno and others were exhorting the composers of new music to write for themselves not for any putative audience, Henze's successes on both concert platform and operatic stage flew in the face of avant-garde sensibilities.

He composed a Second String Quartet (the first dates from 1947) and a Wind Quintet in 1952, his last extended chamber works for over two decades. Until the mid-1970s Henze composed barely a handful of chamber or instrumental pieces that did not use at least one voice. This concentration on vocal music was the outcome of both his theatrical acclaim and the vocal traditions of his new home country. In December 1952, still in Germany, Henze began talking through ideas with Heinz von Cramer for a new opera based on one of Gozzi's plays. Henze's publishers made him a large advance payment on royalties on condition that he resign from the Hesse State Theatre and devote himself to composition. 'I, of course, accepted with gratitude and said "Do you mind if I fulfil your conditions in another country?"' Schott offered no objection and armed also with a Westphalian government grant, Henze crossed the Alps into a new life.

7

New Perspectives 1953–63

Ludwig Erhard, finance minister and architect of West Germany's post-war 'economic miracle'

I seek no cold-blooded cerebral artifice, but rather a thoroughly experienced work of art with a message. Such a work need not be understood for its structural and technical details, but rather for that spiritual message, which is not always automatically expressed in words.

Karl Amadeus Hartmann
on his Seventh Symphony, *Kleine Schriften*

New Perspectives 1953–63

The death of Stalin in March 1953 brought a gradual easing of tension between the capitalist West and Communist East. In Germany, however, no visible changes were detectable. In East Berlin a popular uprising paralysed the city and threatened to spread across the whole of the Democratic Republic before it was put down with brutal efficiency. In the Federal Republic the task of constructing a new society proceeded with a massive building programme and the type of foreign investment that, had it been present in the 1920s, might have averted the rise of the Nazis. Such was the confidence of the newly founded Federal Republic, especially in light of conditions in the east, that there were even calls for rearmament, so that West Germany could play its part in European defence.

When Henze crossed the Italian frontier in 1953 he kept on driving until he reached Venice. There he felt he could safely drink in the Italian atmosphere. He quickly moved on, crossing Tuscany (with a brief stopover near Florence) in a few days. His target was Ischia, the

Cologne, 1962, risen from the ashes thanks to the post-war economic recovery of West Germany

small island in the Bay of Naples which he had visited two years previously. Ischia was still largely undiscovered; a poor fishing community surrounding a small seasonal population of artists – some of whom were of considerable eminence. The self-exiled British composer William Walton had settled there with his Argentine wife, Susana. Also present on the island were the choreographer and director of the Royal Ballet at Covent Garden, Sir Frederick Ashton, and the world-famous poet, Wystan Hugh Auden. The Waltons were permanent residents but Auden, with his companion Chester Kallman, would spend the summer months on Ischia each year, then would go 'back to New York to make money'. Henze rented a tiny cottage – it had no running hot water so he had to visit the local village for a bath – and settled down in this peaceful idyll. He had with him the still incomplete score of *Ode to the West Wind*, his extended instrumental evocation for cello and orchestra of Percy Bysshe Shelley's well-known poem, plus the plan and some sketches for the Gozzi opera, *König Hirsch* ('King Stag').

Despite his absence from Germany, Henze's music was in high demand. *Ein Landarzt* was given a staged production in Cologne in May and Northwest German Radio, which first broadcast the work, wanted another. *Das Ende einer Welt* ('The End of a World') received its première on 4 December. The première of *Ode to the West Wind* took place in Bielefeld on 30 April 1954, and his ballet after Tchaikovsky *Die schlafende Prinzessin* ('The Sleeping Princess') in Essen on 5 June. During this year Henze reduced *Ein Landarzt* to a concert monologue for baritone singer and small orchestra; the radio version was awarded the prestigious Prix d'Italia.

Few of his works caused Henze such effort, or suffered such a chequered history, as *König Hirsch*. Completed late in 1955, it had its first performance during the Berlin Festival on 23 September 1956, in a drastically cut version by Hermann Scherchen. There were noisy demonstrations of approval and opprobrium from the audience for nearly half an hour afterwards. Composer and conductor were held jointly culpable but Henze remained bitter about Scherchen's involvement. That the score was special to him is confirmed by a letter written in January 1973 to Joachim Klaiber: 'It should be seen as a diary, an autobiography, which tells how I discovered music.' Scherchen's pre-eminent place among the avant garde had made

Following page, one of many major new building developments in the recovering Germany: Neue Vahr, near Bremen, built by Gewoba between 1957 and 1962

him aggressive and overbearing; he was known to musicians as the 'Red Dictator'.

In 1955 Henze constructed his Fourth Symphony from the opera's second-act Finale and in 1990, he extracted a further short orchestral work, *La selva incantata* ('The Enchanted Wood'), from the music of the final act. The original version of the opera, which Henze had always preferred, was not performed until May 1985, when the American Dennis Russell Davies conducted it in Stuttgart.

Socially, Henze's three years on Ischia were immensely beneficial. He was invited to a party at Auden's house where he met Walton, who took the young German under his wing. Henze invited Walton and his wife to the première in Naples of *Boulevard Solitude*. 'My dear boy,' he told Henze afterwards, 'in ten years' time you will be a world success.' Stravinsky was also present and, although he later attempted to deny it (for reasons that remain unclear), wrote to Willy Strecker that he found 'incomprehensible the behaviour of part of the audience' and that the performance itself was 'very impressive and full of talent'. In a televised interview Walton singled out Henze as the most talented of the younger generation. The two composers travelled together across Italy to attend performances of operas of mutual interest, such as Prokofiev's *The Fiery Angel*. In December 1954, Walton invited Henze to the première at Covent Garden of his opera, *Troilus and Cressida*. The British immigration authorities refused to allow Henze into the country until Walton had personally vouched for him. On Ischia the Waltons liked to host dinner parties and at one Henze received an extremely unpleasant surprise, as he recalled to the present writer: 'They had a German who had been recommended to them who had just come out of Spandau gaol, Baldur von Schirach, the Nazi leader, as a guest. I left immediately; they didn't know who it was but for me it was the most shocking thing.' As a boy, Henze and his brother Gerhard had had a poster of Hitler on their wall with a motto written by Schirach: 'Each German boy and girl should thank God on their knees every morning that they have got the Führer.' The music-loving Schirach was head of the Hitler Youth, which Henze had been forced to join.

While putting the finishing touches to the opera Henze produced two further orchestral scores which were given their premières by two of the most prestigious international conductors of the day: *Quattro poemi* ('Four Poems') by the American Leopold Stokowski in Frankfurt in May 1955, and *Three Symphonic Studies* by the French conductor and composer Jean Martinon in Hamburg the following February. In January 1956, Henze left Ischia, crossing the Bay to live in Naples itself. The impact of urban Italian life made itself apparent in his music almost immediately, in the more obviously Italianate vocal writing of works such as Five Neapolitan Songs composed straight away for the German baritone, Dietrich Fischer-Dieskau and first performed that May.

Two ballet commissions involved Henze in working with two artists of the highest calibre. *Maratona di danza* ('Dance Marathon') was the idea of Luchino Visconti, best known as a film producer. The ballet deals with a young boy in post-war Rome who is caught up in and killed by the dance marathon craze common to many countries at the time. The music caused Henze difficulty due to the requirement to use jazz for the marathon, and jazz of a sleazy and unimaginative type at that. The second ballet was more conducive to his skills and brought him into contact with Sir Frederick Ashton, who wanted a full evening ballet for Covent Garden. He had originally approached Walton who, smarting from the indifferent reception of *Troilus and Cressida*, suggested Henze as a replacement. The ballet *Undine* was staged in London on 27 October 1958, to Ashton's choreography with Margot Fonteyn in the title role as the water nymph of Friedrich de la Motte-Fouqué's story.

Both *Maratona di danza* and *Undine* provided ammunition for Henze's opponents within the avant garde who felt he had 'betrayed the cause of modern music'. His employment of jazz in the one and Stravinskian, neo-classical elements in the other, led to accusations of stylistic impropriety in that he wavered between different types of music without committing himself to one camp. Henze had in any event become acutely disenchanted with developments at the Darmstadt summer school, to which he had returned in 1955 as a lecturer. Pierre Boulez and Karlheinz Stockhausen had become the driving forces in what was by then the powerhouse of experimental music. Henze had little sympathy with their aesthetic and in turn they demonstrated their disapproval of his music in 1958 by pointedly walking out of the first performance of *Nachtstücke und Arien* ('Nocturnes and Arias') at Donaueschingen.

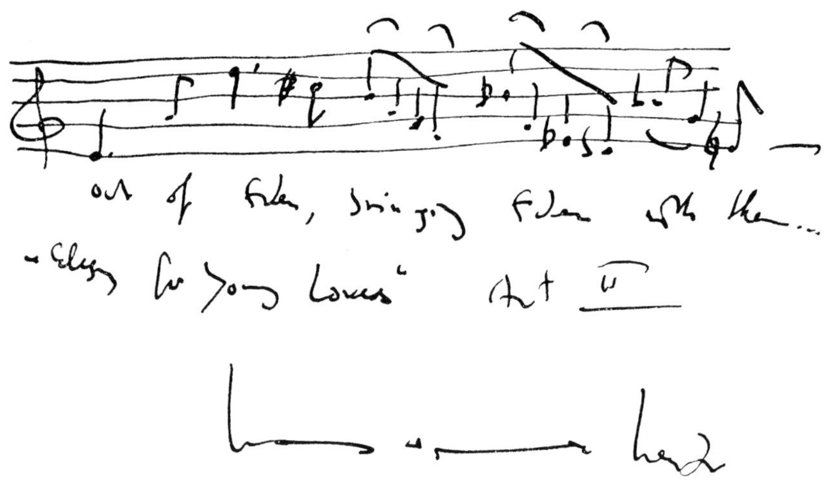

Above, 'Out of Eden, bringing Eden with them ...', a sketch signed by Henze of his setting of the opening words from Mittenhofer's poem 'The Young Lovers' from Act Two of his opera, *Elegy for Young Lovers*, 1961. *Left*, Henze in a 1961 BBC radio interview with W. H. Auden and Chester Kallman, the librettists of *Elegy for Young Lovers* (and of *The Bassarids* in 1964)

Nachtstücke und Arien was a set of orchestral pieces encompassing settings of two poems by the Austrian poetess, Ingeborg Bachmann, who helped adapt the libretto for Henze's next opera, *Der Prinz von Homburg* ('The Prince of Homburg'), from the play by Heinrich von Kleist. The initial suggestion had come from Visconti, but Kleist's story of the individual caught by and defying the machinery of the State, possessed a real and pertinent appeal to the composer, both in the wider context of German political life as well as in his relationship to the musical establishment. Henze's music fell between two stools: too adventurous for the conservative press and the bulk of opera-loving audiences (which did not stop them turning out to hear it), it was also not radical enough for the pioneers. *Der Prinz von Homburg* was, however, staged right across Germany in most of the leading, and many lesser, opera houses, becoming more viable commercially than any of its predecessors. Henze had taken great pains with this score, for the first time working out many of the compositional problems in smaller-scale, satellite works. These included *Kammermusik 1958*, the orchestral *Three Dithyrambs*, sonatas for string orchestra and for piano, and the pantomime *Des Kaisers Nachtigall* ('The Emperor's Nightingale'). *Kammermusik 1958* is totally unlike Hindemith's works of the 1920s, being not a concerto but an extended song-cycle for tenor, guitar and eight other performers, setting Friedrich Hölderlin's 'In Lovely Blueness'. The cycle was composed during a visit to Greece, the inspiration also for Hölderlin's fragmentary poems, to a commission from North German Radio. It was dedicated to another English composer, Benjamin Britten, as 'a true act of homage and an expression of gratitude for the inspiration that his works have given me'. Henze had encountered Britten's music in 1946 with *Peter Grimes* and was particularly impressed with the four 'Sea Interludes', often performed separately as a concert suite. The two composers later struck up a cordial relationship, Britten returning the compliment by dedicating his setting of Brecht's *Children's Crusade* to Henze in 1968. Five years after completing *Kammermusik 1958*, Henze added a purely instrumental epilogue celebrating the seventieth birthday of Josef Rufer, a disciple of Schoenberg. (Rufer's writings on twelve-note composition had been widely praised and had even made a favourable impression on Hindemith.) The three guitar interludes, or *Tentos*, from

Kammermusik 1958 were in addition published separately and have enjoyed success independently in the recital room.

In 1959, Henze linked up with his erstwhile neighbour on Ischia (and Britten's former collaborator), W. H. Auden. Whilst on the island, Henze had been in awe of both Auden and Kallman, still fresh from their triumph with Stravinsky in *The Rake's Progress*. 'When I lived there,' Henze confided, 'I saw them quite a lot but I still didn't have the courage to ask them [about a possible collaboration]. Years later when I had left Ischia I wrote to them in New York ... and the answer was affirmative.' The result was another opera, *Elegy for Young Lovers*, and occupied Henze from 1959 until 1961. The opera takes its title from a poem which is about to be declaimed publicly as the opera ends. If heard, the poem would recount the tragic events of the opera as a further example of the manipulative poet Mittenhofer's subjugation of the lives – and deaths – of those around him to the service of his art. *Elegy for Young Lovers* was first performed in a German translation in Schwetzingen on 20 May 1961. Inevitably, comparisons were drawn with *The Rake's Progress* and both music and libretto were often found wanting. Writing in 1964, Wolf-Eberhard von Lewinski found the opera 'so complex and unusual in terms of plot that it does not draw the favour of the larger public'. This did not prevent the work from being rapidly taken up in Switzerland, Germany and Britain and becoming something of a modern classic. So pleased with it were the librettists that they immediately suggested to Henze a new opera, to be based on the ancient Greek drama, *The Bacchae*, by Euripides. *Elegy for Young Lovers* also provoked an irreconcilable row between Stockhausen and Herbert Eimert, the director of the electronic studio in Cologne where Stockhausen worked. Eimert had reported back of his delight with Henze's music; Stockhausen considered it anathema.

Henze moved from Naples to Rome in 1961, where he received a commission from the New York Philharmonic Orchestra for a new symphony – his fifth. He completed it in 1962 and it was premièred the following May by Leonard Bernstein. He completed the recomposition of the early First Symphony as a three-movement chamber work, conducting its first performance in April 1964 with the Berlin Philharmonic. Henze had begun to develop a closer relationship with this orchestra following a commission for a short orchestral piece in 1959, *Antifone*, given its première by Herbert von Karajan in January 1962. The same orchestra finally gave the much-delayed first performance, under Henze's direction, of the Fourth Symphony during the Berlin Festival in October 1963.

Henze's principal preoccupation was still with the human voice. *Ariosi* is a group of five songs for soprano, solo violin and orchestra (the composer later made a version for piano, four hands) to words by the medieval Italian poet, Torquato Tasso. In *Ariosi* Henze further refined the delicate melodic writing that had characterized the Neapolitan Songs, *Nachtstücke und Arien* and *Kammermusik 1958*. He next turned to the poems of the Frenchman, Arthur Rimbaud (set by Britten in his song-cycle *Les Illuminations*) with the cantata *Being Beauteous*, perhaps the ultimate refinement of his vocal style of his first ten years in Italy. Henze also produced two choral works, the fifty-minute cantata *Novae de infinito laudes* ('New Praises of the Infinite', 1962) and the more modest *Cantata della fiaba estrema* ('Song of the Final Fairy-tale', 1963). *Novae de infinito laudes* set texts by the sixteenth-century Italian writer Giordano Bruno. Commissioned by the London Philharmonic Society, it was too expensive to rehearse even with a reduced orchestra and its eventual première, on 24 April 1963, took place at the Venice Biennale festival with Elisabeth Söderström, Kerstin Meyer, Peter Pears and Fischer-Dieskau. Among the audience were Britten and the visibly ailing Hartmann, whose Eighth Symphony was first performed during this same festival. The celebrity of performers and audience alone was a measure of Henze's stature in his late thirties in the world of music.

Unlike Hindemith and Henze, Hartmann remained a slow and fastidious composer who derived aesthetic pleasure from the graphic presentation of his scores as well as from their content. The regeneration of musical life in Germany involved the bestowing of awards and prizes, partly in encouragement of new talent, partly out of guilt with the past. Hartmann was a major beneficiary. In 1949 he was awarded the music prize of the city of Munich. In the following year he received the art prize of the Bavarian Academy of Fine Arts, which in 1953 elected him as a member. In 1954 he was the recipient of the Schoenberg Medal of the International Society for Contemporary Music (ISCM) and in 1955 was elected as a member of the Berlin Academy of Arts. Further awards continued, at about one per year, for the remainder of his life. Hindemith and Henze were similarly endowed. In the same year as Hartmann's election to the Berlin Academy, Hindemith received the prestigious Wihuri-Sibelius prize which carried an award of approximately three times his annual salary from Zurich University. All three composers received the North Rhineland-Westphalia Arts prize, Henze in 1956, Hartmann the following year and Hindemith in 1958. This last award seems to have pricked Hindemith into an uncharacteristically sour response. Whether he felt slighted at receiving it only after his younger compatriots, or felt that the sheer volume of prizes being awarded devalued the whole system of awards, his acid remark in a letter to Ludwig Strecker denigrating 'the Ruhr coal and pumpernickel prize' is out of character.

The Musica Viva concerts occupied Hartmann throughout the 1950s. Quite apart from the programming of the concerts he gave consideration to their presentation, as his letters of these years attest. Artists who contributed pictures or designs for posters and programme books included Marc Chagall, Jean Cocteau, Le Corbusier, Helmut Jürgens (who designed the scenery for the 1960 staging of *Simplicius Simplicissimus* in Munich), Kokoschka, Ewald Mataré, Georges Mathieu, Marino Marini, Joan Miró and Picasso. Hartmann steadfastly maintained the unapologetic radicalism of the concerts and displayed an unusual flexibility over content. Where possible he would take on works which could not be programmed elsewhere. In 1953 he took on board at short notice Stockhausen's *Schlagquartett* ('Percussion Quartet') for piano and timpani after Hamburg Radio had refused to broadcast it. Hartmann was not above learning from works that he included. The music of Boris Blacher featured consistently in the Musica Viva programmes. Blacher's systematic use of variable metres, the rhythms evolving bar-by-bar from numerical progressions, made a great impression on Hartmann's compositions.

Important features of Musica Viva year by year were reappraisals of music written earlier in the century, or by composers of pre-war repute who had been, like himself, lost in the post-war crush. Hindemith was invited to conduct on several occasions during the 1950s and Hartmann did not make the mistake made by many festival and orchestral managers by booking him to conduct just his own music. Hartmann's suggested programme for a concert of wind

Opposite, Erich Auerbach's quintessential portrait of the young Henze with cigarette, 1963

Musica viva
Strawinsky · Choral-Variationen · Psalmen Symphonie
das Augenlicht · Webern · Ricercata
Nono · Varianti
20 Uhr
Kolisch · Scherchen
Herkulessaal · 24 · Jan · Freitag

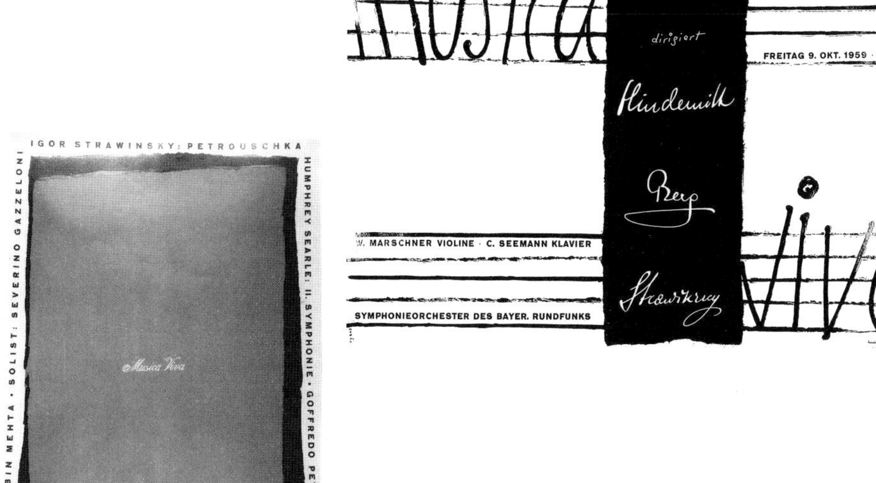

The artistic legacy of Musica Viva – concert posters which Hartmann commissioned from Helmut Jürgens: 1958, *left*; 1959, *right*; 1962, *above*

orchestra works for the 1959 season included two pieces of Hindemith's – *Konzertmusik*, Op. 41, and Symphony in B flat – but added two more challenging scores: Berg's Chamber Concerto for piano, violin and thirteen wind instruments and Stravinsky's *Symphonies of Wind Instruments – In Memoriam Debussy*. Hartmann was also keen to bring Darius Milhaud to Munich, as the latter's widow Madeleine recalls:

DM was invited to conduct in Munich in 1957. It would have been his first concert in Germany since the war. Unfortunately he was sick and Dr Hartmann invited Manuel Rosenthal ... to conduct my husband's works. In 1962 K. A. Hartmann invited DM again – a few weeks before the concert he fell on his knees and he was in pain day and night. But he decided to go to Munich all the same. It was not easy but Hartmann was an Engel *[Mme Milhaud used the German word for angel]. He found two nurses who helped Darius to reach the theatre and the podium, etc. He had our meals brought to the concert hall so that DM would not have to go out between two rehearsals. I am sorry to say that we were not able to see Dr Hartmann thereafter. He was a* marvellous Human Being*!*

The première of Hartmann's Sixth Symphony, which quickly followed its completion, was given on 24 April 1953, by the Bavarian Radio Orchestra conducted by Eugen Jochum. Hartmann then turned to composing his first original pieces since the war. The Concerto for Piano, Wind Instruments and Percussion is a work of electric vitality and reflects the more recent influences on his style, not least Blacher's. The configuration of the work stems in part from Bartók's *Music for Strings, Percussion and Celesta* of 1936 and Sonata for Two Pianos and Percussion of two years later. Hartmann's concerto was unveiled in Donaueschingen almost as soon as the ink was dry by the Southwest German Radio Orchestra under Rosbaud, with Maria Bergman as the solo pianist. Its success encouraged Hartmann to tackle another when he received a commission from Hesse Radio, adding a solo viola to the Piano Concerto's ensemble. It is on a much bigger scale, nearly twice the length of the Piano Concerto, and the dimensions are a testimony to the composer's growing confidence. It also took twice as long to write, not reaching completion until 1956. The work is truly a viola concerto, the piano being used rather more as an orchestral instrument than in the earlier work. The concerto was dedicated to William Primrose, the famous Anglo-American virtuoso for whom Bartók had begun his concerto shortly before his death in 1945. The first performance was given in Frankfurt am Main on 25 May 1956, with Jascha Vleissi deputizing for Primrose (who was ill) in the solo viola part and Annemarie Bohne playing the piano.

Hartmann could not entirely give up the tendency to revisit earlier works. He again looked over his settings of Walt Whitman for alto and orchestra, *Versuch eines Requiems*, and produced a new version for Vienna in June 1955 which created a big impression and put Hartmann back before an international audience for the first time since Collaer's pre-war performances. In 1956 Hartmann set out to revamp his largest work of all, the opera *Des Simplicius Simplicissimus Jugend*. He did so at the instigation of the Swiss composer Rolf Liebermann, to whom his Fourth Symphony had been inscribed. Hartmann simplified the opera's title to *Simplicius Simplicissimus* and

Recalled by Madame Milhaud as 'a marvellous Human Being!': Karl Amadeus Hartmann in his music study, late 1950s

removed a few short episodes. He expanded the orchestra required to in excess of fifty musicians, in the main adding to the strings and percussion. The original's use of single brass and woodwind (with no oboe, horn or tuba) remained. The new version was produced in Mannheim in July 1957 with scenery by Joachim Klaiber.

Hartmann's position in German musical life was full of contradictions. As a composer, he was essentially a Bavarian celebrity, but his personal integrity and service in the cause of new music made his name known across the country and beyond. The works that received their first public performances in the late 1940s and 1950s possessed a surface aggression and dynamic energy that was quintessentially twentieth century in inspiration, with a sound world obviously influenced by Berg and more radical elements. Yet Hartmann's music remained tonally based. On musical grounds, if Henze's music was unacceptable to the Darmstadt avant garde then Hartmann's should have been still further beyond the pale, yet on the whole he was exonerated by the experimentalists. Even the fact that he was first and foremost a composer of symphonies – at a time when the symphony as a genre was held to be moribund – does not seem to have attracted adverse criticism. As an administrator he was liked by the radicals. As a composer, they preferred not to refer to him at all. The Finnish composer, Paavo Heininen, studied with Bernd Alois Zimmermann in Cologne during 1961. Heininen recalls:

Zimmermann never mentioned Hartmann. But practically nobody ever mentioned Hartmann at that time. I was an eager collector of

Recriminations at Berlin's east–west divide: 'Concentration-camp architect Lübke [president of West Germany, 1959-69], how much longer will you lie?'

US troops on alert at a Berlin border checkpoint during the height of the Cold War, 1961

recordings ... of radio broadcasts of the many German networks, but my harvest of Hartmann was very meagre (Symphonies II and VII). That was the time of most ardent serialism, so I remember the name of Hartmann mentioned just once – by chance, at the occasion of a performance of 'a' symphony, conducted by 'der' Zillig [the composer Winfried Zillig] – and the symphony was 'not so bad'. I preferred not to mention my great enthusiasm.

Hartmann's Sixth Symphony was featured at an ISCM festival in Zurich in 1957 and received its North American première in 1959, conducted by the long-serving director of the Philadelphia Orchestra, Eugene Ormandy. Symphony No. 7 was unveiled that same year as the result of a request from the Serge Koussevitsky Music Foundation. Hartmann's Eighth and final Symphony followed on more or less immediately to commission from West German Radio. He was approached over a plan to present his Seventh Symphony as a ballet. He acquiesced but was unhappy about the political scenario, as set out in a letter to the choreographer, Heinz Rosen, on 14 November: 'I ... do not wish to see my political conscience displayed on stage and am of the opinion that the expression of an artist's political opinions can only be expressed indirectly, and not directly as if on placards.' In

Following page, Berlin in 1964, a divided city of sundered families

1960 he was approached by Dessau and Henze to contribute a movement to a composite work entitled *Judische Chronik* ('Jewish Chronicle'), a public reaction at the re-awakening of anti-Semitism in Germany just fifteen years after the Holocaust. With neo-Nazi desecration of Jewish cemeteries and synagogues Jens Gerlach was engaged to produce a suitable text and Hartmann's contribution was entitled *Ghetto*, scored for alto and baritone solo singers with a small orchestra and evoking the terrors of the Nazi ghettos of the 1940s. The other movements were written individually by Dessau, Henze, Blacher and Rudolf Wagner-Régeny. Hartmann completed *Ghetto* in 1961, but *Judische Chronik* was not heard until 14 January 1966, since Hartmann witheld permission for its performance. Henze believed this decision to be connected with the erection of the Berlin Wall, perhaps due to a wish on Hartmann's part not to be seen 'collaborating' with composers from the Democratic Republic. 'A political decision of very poor ground,' Henze recollects, 'when if two composers were from East Germany one of them was a Jew and the other was Wagner-Régeny, a gentleman to whom the idea of racism was painful. Hartmann made the performances impossible at a moment when they were of the greatest urgency.' Elisabeth Hartmann is categoric that there was 'no connection between the building of the Berlin Wall and the delayed performance of *Ghetto*'. It may well be that Hartmann's delay in releasing *Ghetto* was due to ill-health. In 1962 he underwent surgery for throat-cancer.

Hartmann's final composition was *Gesangsszene* ('Hymn-scene'), a setting for baritone and orchestra of an apocalyptic extract from Jean Giraudoux's *Sodom und Gomorrha*. (Hartmann had contemplated a work based on the same writer's *Undine* in 1933 but nothing concrete came of it.) In its concerns with environmental issues – deeply untopical at that time – and committed political stance (in the widest sense), *Gesangsszene* was prophetic of the areas into which composers – Henze not least – would enter later in the decade. The text's references to atomic power and the destruction of natural resources have with the passage of the years served to reinforce the work's relevance; the reference to cancer as a disease of civilization was to have a tragic irony. Hartmann set to work, while the Eighth Symphony was still unfinished, on *Gesangsszene*, but did not live to complete it. He died, aged fifty-seven, from carcinoma of the stomach on 5 December 1963 with the last nine lines unset. The final two:

This is an end of the world
The saddest of them all!

were intended to be spoken after the music had stopped, so the work has been performed as it stands.

After Hartmann's death, a new director had to be found to take charge of Musica Viva. 'The question of who was to be Hartmann's successor as director,' recalls Elisabeth Hartmann 'was settled by the director of programmes, Cube, who insisted on a composer. This is why Wolfgang Fortner was appointed.' Not everyone had cause to be thankful. Fortner may have tried to perpetuate Hartmann's adventurous programming, but accessibility to the concerts themselves was an early victim of the new regime. The British composer John McCabe had travelled to Munich for a year's post-graduate work in 1964. His original intention was to study with Hartmann but he 'said he did not teach. What he would do would be to recommend a teacher to me, who was Harald Genzmer ... and Hartmann would supervise by seeing me once a month.' In the interim Hartmann died but McCabe still studied with Genzmer, who had been a pupil of Hindemith in Berlin. The great concert series was closed to him while he was there, since the special seats for students, rigorously maintained by Hartmann, had been abolished. 'Fortner ... stopped all that,' McCabe recollects. 'I was never able to go to a Musica Viva concert the year I was there. It was *the* thing to go to; socialites would sit through a concert of Luigi Nono and not have the faintest idea what was going on. But that was what it was all about.'

Hindemith, established at Zurich University, found a permanent home in the village of Blonay, near Vevey. Once installed, the Hindemiths set about collecting their widely dispersed belongings from America and Germany and were amazed to find that much of their furniture from the pre-war Berlin flat had survived. After losing money on his initial return trips to Europe after the war, Hindemith pushed himself more and more into conducting. This took time away from composition and had a derogatory effect on his health. As he passed sixty years he found his schedule too taxing. He gave up teaching at Zurich and resisted all inducements from Yale to return. If he felt that work on the Kepler opera, *Die Harmonie der Welt*, was his overriding priority, criss-crossing Europe – and indeed other continents, including a tour of Japan with the Vienna Philharmonic – was hardly the most productive of life-styles. In truth, he was piqued that he did not receive more conducting engagements in the USA and felt that he was undervalued there. As an American citizen of some celebrity travelling the world he felt ignored when the diplomatic staff of his adopted country neglected his concerts in the nations he visited. In his last years Hindemith hankered after the status of a 'great man'. It did not affect his conduct 'at work'. The composer and BBC producer Robert Simpson found him 'a genial character, a real musician with no air of self-importance'. Yet the success of his music failed to satisfy Hindemith's inner self. He was pleased enough to record his own pieces, as in London in November 1956, setting down the Horn Concerto (with Dennis Brain as soloist), the suite from *Nobilissima Visione*, *Konzertmusik*, Op. 50, and Symphony in B flat for wind orchestra, but as a conductor he demanded to be taken seriously in mainstream repertoire. For him, this extended from Bach to Bartók. Hindemith's performances did not always elicit critical approval. When in October 1958 he stood in for an indisposed Otto Klemperer to conduct Beethoven's Ninth Symphony in London, there was 'a positive outcry against Hindemith's Beethoven'. Several of his students present at the concert took a different view, out of their knowledge of and loyalty to their former teacher. The composer Arnold Cooke described it as 'an early-eighteenth-century view of the work, practical and without apocalyptic climaxes'. Franz Reizenstein went rather further in his obituary for Hindemith in January 1964, recalling it as 'the most lucid exposition of this score that I have ever heard'.

Hindemith composed just eleven works in the last ten years of his life. These included the final instrumental sonata, for bass tuba and piano, in 1955 and his sixth and final symphony, known as the 'Pittsburgh' Symphony, in 1958. Aspects of these two works have given rise to speculation that Hindemith might have been contemplating a partial adoption of serial techniques into his music. This would have been a remarkable volte face for a composer who had been unequivocal in his rejection of Schoenberg's method. The flimsy evidence for this is the repetitive treatment of certain note-patterns, along with the orchestration of parts of the 'Pittsburgh' Symphony, which has been said to resemble the pointillist instrumentation used by Webern in many of his later works. However, from a knowledge of the orchestral sound of American composers of the period – such as Roy Harris, William Schuman or Walter Piston – the relevant passages can just as easily be heard as a wholly characteristic intent to create an American sound (for Hindemith) when writing for an American orchestra. Hindemith's attitude to serialism remained doggedly unenthusiastic. In the 1953 German edition of *A Composer's World*, Hindemith reiterated his view on atonality: 'What is held to be "atonality" necessarily turns out to be another aspect of tonality – the only difference being that the "atonal" work fixes the sequences in another of the various corners of the full tonal area.' Hindemith was never interested in exploring such 'corners of the full tonal area' himself; indeed, it is not impossible that his apparent flirtations were serialism were in fact heavy-handed and not overly successful jokes at the avant

Hindemith embarks on an international conducting career, including an engagement at the temple of Wagnerian Opera, Bayreuth, 1953

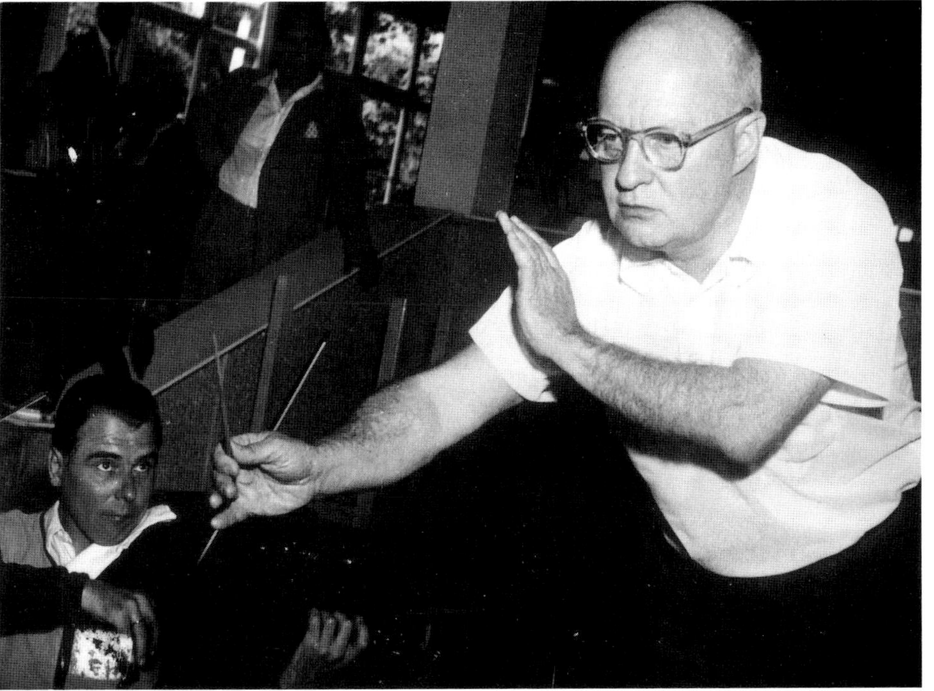

garde's expense. This did not restrict his keen interest in new means of expression, as shown by his desire to visit the controversial electronic studio in Cologne, where Stockhausen played Hindemith one of his electronic studies. The latter was not impressed. 'He did not utter a single, printable word, and off he went.' Stockhausen was shocked because he 'respected [Hindemith] as a master craftsman,

A Christmas card drawn by Hindemith. The lion probably symbolizes Gertrud, whose zodiacal sign was Leo.It reads: '1958 Best wishes for Christmas and the New Year 1959'.

had played his works and knew and greatly admired the *Marienleben* and *Mathis der Maler*. I was thus disappointed that this man simply denied my musicality.'

The main composition of Hindemith's last years was *Die Harmonie der Welt*. Only in 1956 did Hindemith finally complete the libretto to his satisfaction and by May of the next year the music was finished. As an opera dealing with the relationship of the artist to the world about him, *Die Harmonie der Welt* can be seen as the culmination of the concerns central to *Cardillac* and *Mathis der Maler*. In some ways *Die Harmonie der Welt* is Hindemith's magnum opus, into which he poured his lifetime's experience and theoretical consideration. The failure of its première in 1957, which he conducted, was a great disappointment to him. Despite a second, more successful production in Bremen that year, the opera has not entered the modern repertoire. Lacking the clear-cut dramatic issues of these earlier operas, *Die Harmonie der Welt* gives the impression of a philosophical discourse not entirely suited to the theatre.

Hindemith's inclination to compose was at a low ebb. He prepared an edition of Reger's *Psalm 100* for chorus and orchestra, and composed a routine Octet for Clarinet, Bassoon, Horn, Violin, Two Violas, Cello and Double Bass. This failed to excite much attention even though the composer made a rare appearance as a violist at the première. In 1960 came another opera, the hour-long, one-act *The Long Christmas Dinner*, to a libretto by Thornton Wilder and based on his stage play. Although discussions were held about a companion piece (and Hindemith consulted several other writers in case Wilder should fail to provide a libretto), both librettist and composer died before these plans could be realized. In 1961 Hindemith tinkered yet again with *Cardillac*. A cantata *Mainzer Umzug* ('The Procession of Mainz') was written for the two-thousandth anniversary of the foundation of the city of Mainz; a fine new Concerto for Organ and Orchestra was performed by the organist and composer, Anton Heiller, who championed it across the world. Hindemith's final work, completed late in 1963, was a setting of the Roman Catholic Mass for unaccompanied chorus. It was not the result of any religious sentiment or conversion, nor even from the promptings of the devout Gertrud. Mass settings were a prominent feature of German musical life from the medieval period on, and the composition of one was simply another manifestation of Hindemith's connection with his musical roots. A few days after its première, Hindemith fell ill. A workaholic for most of his adult life, overwork had exhausted him. December 1963 was a catastrophic month for German music. Hartmann's death on the 5th was followed a fortnight later by Winfried Zillig's. Hindemith, after a series of strokes, died in his sleep of pancreatitis on 28 December at the age of sixty-eight. Of the lineage of outstanding German symphonists, Henze alone survived – on the one hand as the future exponent of German traditions, on the other as their most outspoken dissident.

8

The Politics of Commitment 1963–

Hans Werner Henze in the 1960s

In my world the old [musical] forms strive to regain significance even when the new sounds, the modern timbre of the music seldom or never permits them to rise to the surface … [they] appear to me as classical ideals of beauty, no longer attainable but still visible from a great distance, arousing memories like dreams.

Henze, *Instrumental Composition,* lecture delivered at Berlin Technical University, January 1963

The Politics of Commitment 1963–

Even had Hindemith and Hartmann lived beyond December 1963 it is most unlikely that either could have eclipsed Henze in terms of public and critical acclaim. The works of Hindemith that had entered the general repertoire were restricted to a limited period in his career, from about 1930 to 1945 (exceptions being the instrumental sonatas, which were assured a permanent place in the recital repertoire). Where scholarly interest was shown it was directed – much to Hindemith's annoyance – at his more radical music of the 1920s, most of which he had disowned and was content to forget. The relative failure of his later projects, including the last two technical books and most particularly the opera *Die Harmonie der Welt*, stood in marked contrast to the attention-snatching success of Henze's younger, more aggressive music.

Henze fulfilled one of Auden's principal preparatory requirements for *The Bassarids* – being forced to sit through all five hours of Wagner's *Götterdämmerung* ('Twilight of the Gods'). He duly received the libretto late in 1963 but, much as he admired the text, he set it aside to tackle first a comic opera, *Der junge Lord* ('The Young Lord') to a libretto by Ingeborg Bachmann. She provided 'the best libretto I've ever had. Difficult to get the lyrics out of her; one had to resort to rather unconventional ways.' This involved locking her up in a top-floor room in Henze's house in Marino and not letting her out – even to eat – until her daily quota was achieved. Even severe toothache was treated by the composer with suspicion; he took her to the dentist, but all the treatment had to be completed there and then.

In keeping with the classical poise of Bachmann's text, Henze consciously looked to the operas of Rossini, in particular *Il barbiere di Siviglia* ('The Barber of Seville'), and Mozart, especially, *Così fan tutte* ('So Do All Women') and *Die Entführung aus dem Serail* ('The Abduction from the Harem'). Henze employed an orchestra of early nineteenth-century dimensions, with a twentieth-century-sized percussion section. The result was one of his most balanced and appealing compositions, a perfect evocation of Classical opera without once demeaning itself in simple pastiche. And although this is a comic opera, there is a hard edge to it. Not all the characters deserving of a happy ending receive one. The setting in the imaginary Hülsdorf-Gotha is characterized by a physical poverty and hunger that is a metaphor for spiritual inadequacy.

The première of *Der junge Lord* at the Deutsche Oper, in Berlin on 7 April 1965, was Henze's most complete success to date. Thunderous applause greeted the production and opera houses vied with each other to mount the work. Walton's prophecy in 1954 after hearing *Boulevard Solitude* that in ten years' time Henze would be a 'world success' was vindicated. His main preoccupation now was the music for *The Bassarids*. This was written at white-hot speed 'in a spirit of protest with no properly reasoned basis, and in great isolation'. Unfocused as this may have been, part at least of the protest was occasioned by the various terms and conditions imposed by Auden and Kallman, which included a requirement for a tiny musical quote from Bach's St Matthew Passion. These impositions proved a stimulating force, although it took several years for Henze to appreciate this. The impact of Wagner, demanded by the librettists, led him to conceive the opera in symphonic terms (the four tableaux of what is a single-act opera correspond to the four movements of the conventional symphony). In doing so Henze synthesized many elements of his musical language in ways unparalleled in his output. The updated and symbolic allegory derived from the ancient tragedy of the royal house of Thebes embraced the prime concern of the relationship of the individual to the state expressed diversely in *König Hirsch*, *Der Prinz von Homburg* and *Der junge Lord*. Even *Elegy for Young Lovers*, Henze's previous collaboration with Auden and Kallman, has a related theme, albeit on a domestic level, arising from the conflicts of the characters with the martinet poet, Mittenhofer.

The Bassarids was produced at the Salzburg Festival in August 1966, just five weeks after its composer's fortieth birthday. The opera was conducted by Christoph von Dohnányi who directed the première of *Der junge Lord* the year before. *The Bassarids* attracted still more attention, assuring Henze's occupation of the centre-stage of mainstream composition, not just in Germany. Yet this apogee of worldly success precipitated in his music a crisis that would require a radical, external solution.

Henze with producer G. R. Sellner (on the left), preparing the staging of his Euripidean opera *The Bassarids* for its Salzburg première, 1966

The causes of this crisis, of which Henze was becoming dimly aware whilst composing *The Bassarids*, were private and personal. In the late 1950s he had allowed his practical musical horizons to be widened. More and more often he permitted himself to look up from the writing desk and pick up the conductor's baton, first in his own works, then in Brahms, Beethoven, Mahler. In 1961 he was appointed professor of composition at the Mozarteum in Salzburg and conducted a master class there until 1967. On 28 January 1963, he delivered a memorable lecture at Berlin University, discussing musical aesthetics and the relationship of art with politics. Henze finally took a more overtly public stance when he joined with other intellectuals (including the writer Günter Grass) to campaign on behalf of Willi Brandt, a Socialist former refugee from the Nazis, in the 1965 presidential election 'but with a feeling of impotence and uselessness'. This expansion of view and action contrasted with what Henze regarded as an implosion of his music's expressive target. His art 'was becoming more and more private, ... its motivations were private ones, ... it contained private communications'. For a composer committed to reaching the largest audience possible, who had rejected the Darmstadt philosophy of defying the public, such a realization came as a terrible shock. 'All at once I felt that I did not understand anything any more, that I had nothing, that I was cut off.' The uncertainty of artistic goal was reflected in his music during 1966 and 1967. One manifestation of this uncertainty was the re-emergence of prominent non-vocal compositions: the concertos for oboe and harp (1966), double bass (1966) and the enormous, exploratory Second Piano Concerto (1967). Even *Musen Siziliens*, a half-hour-long choral setting of fragmentary texts by the Roman poet Virgil, is styled a concerto for chorus, two pianos, wind and timpani. A film score, for Volker Schlöndorff's *Der junge Törless*, after Robert Musil's novel of juvenile homosexuality, yielded one of Henze's most popular instrumental items, the *Fantasia for Strings* (performable either as a sextet or for orchestra).

The solution to his aesthetic impasse when it came, drew on several causes and experiences. Henze visited Japan in 1966 to conduct *Elegy for Young Lovers* and encountered the native, ritual Gagaku music of the royal court. He visited the USA for the first time to attend the 1963 world première of his Fifth Symphony and New York had made a definite impact on him. On a return trip in 1967 as a visiting professor of music in New Hampshire, Henze became profoundly stirred by the anti-Vietnam protests and the campaigns for civil rights and racial equality. Back in Germany, these same issues were bringing the students out on to the streets to demonstrate and reject established authority. The tension this engendered became more poignant with the death of a student protester in June 1967 during a demonstration against a visit by the Shah of Iran, Mohammed Reza Pahlavi. The way suddenly became clear for the composer. Berlin, the city where Henze most craved approval, was host to the vanguard of the younger generation's anti-authoritarian resistance, crystallized in the extra-parliamentary opposition led by Rudi Dutschke. Henze went to meet him and offer his services to the cause: 'I wanted to make myself of use to these young people.'

The actions of the students were viewed with deep suspicion by the government of West Berlin as well as older members of the population. Both were constantly on guard against hostile action from across the border with the surrounding territory of the Communist Democratic Republic. Memories of the Berlin blockade during the late 1940s and the sudden erection of the Wall in 1961 left the more conservative echelons of society resistant and antagonistic to the left-wing sympathies of the students. The Wall was an oppressive, ever-present reminder of the city's isolation. The British timpanist and conductor Gary Brain studied in Berlin during 1967–8 at the Hochschule. He recalls the atmosphere:

At the end of the street where I lived ... in the beautiful woods of the Nikolassee, ran the famous Wall. During summer months when supping and drinking wine with my landlady in the early evening, there would be frequent thunderstorms. During these, Frau Schlokow used to say, 'They will try the Wall tonight.' They [prospective escapees from East Berlin] certainly often did as in the noisiest moments of the tempest, flares would go up and the sound of machine guns wiped out nature's noise.

As with the Berlin of the 1930s, violence and shootings were counterpointed by artistic excellence:

It was the period of Karajan at his best. Whatever is said about the man when he was good he was very, very good. His Bruckner and his Debussy, Henze and Hindemith are etched in my mind forever.

The crucial year was 1968. Student unrest, centred on Paris and Berlin, had spread right across Western Europe and to the USA. The failure of governments and national institutions to cope with the mood of the protest movement only inflamed the conflict further. With Paul Dessau, Henze resigned from the Berlin Academy in protest at its rejecting membership for the Berlin-based Korean composer Isang Yun, whose political involvements had rendered him unacceptable. In 1967 Yun and his wife were abducted by South Korean secret police and forcibly repatriated to stand trial on trumped-up charges of sedition and spying. Yun was sentenced to life imprisonment and his wife received three years. European musicians were incensed and petitioned for his release and return to Germany. Active in the campaign apart from Henze and Dessau were musicians as different and aesthetically opposed as Boulez, Klemperer, Stockhausen and Stravinsky. Yun was eventually released in 1969.

Having quit the Academy in the Federal Republic, Henze underlined his dissent by becoming a member of the corresponding

'I wanted to make myself of use to these young people.' Henze actively supported the student protest movement, shown here in Bonn, 1973, demonstrating at the visit of Soviet Premier Leonid Brezhnev. In 1968, a demonstration hijacked the Hamburg première of Henze's *The Raft of the 'Medusa'*, causing a riot.

Academy in the Democratic Republic. This was not his only act of solidarity; at Easter, an attempt was made to assassinate Dutschke. Henze sheltered him afterwards in Marino, watching in dismay the simultaneous rise in the polls of the neo-Nazi NDP, who captured ten per cent of the vote in Baden-Württemburg that month.

A collision with the establishment was inevitable. It occurred at the première in Hamburg on 9 December 1968, of his 'vulgar and military' oratorio, *Das Floss der »Medusa«* ('The Raft of the "Medusa"'). The work was written as a political requiem for Ernesto 'Che' Guevara, the revolutionary who had been executed by the Bolivian government in October 1967. Henze incorporated the names of several martyred freedom fighters from the under-developed countries into the text, which was written by Ernest Schnabel and based on a real historical event. In 1816 the frigate *Medusa* had foundered off the coast of Senegal. The captain, officers and other dignitaries aboard (including priests) deserted the crew and passengers – who numbered some three hundred men, women and children. The crew attempted to sail home on an enormous, makeshift raft, but with almost no provisions only a handful survived. All Europe was scandalized by the incident, the moment of rescue being immortalized in Géricault's great canvas. This painting acted as a direct inspiration for the music's character.

The trouble at the first performance of Henze's oratorio started before a note of the music was heard in the auditorium. Groups of

Henze (on the right) in 1965 with his revered composer colleague Paul Dessau, a 'Marxist and humanistic moralist' and posthumous dedicatee of *Barcarola*

Right, Géricault's monumental canvas *The Raft of the 'Medusa'* depicts the abandoned survivors of the foundered frigate 'Medusa'. It was the inspiration for Henze's 'vulgar and military' oratorio of the same name.

left-wing students showered the audience with leaflets protesting against materialism, the consumer culture and various political causes. A poster of Guevara was put up on the podium, only to be torn down and ripped up by the local director of radio who had organized the concert. The students retaliated by placing a red flag on stage. This provoked complaints from members of the chorus and an appeal was made to Henze to remove it. The composer, while not linked to the demonstration in the hall, was not unsympathetic towards it and just wanted to conduct his music. Part of the chorus duly left the stage in counter-protest and a furious row ensued, settled only by the intervention of armed police. Large numbers of people were arrested and beaten, including Schnabel the librettist. The concert had to be abandoned as Henze felt it immoral to proceed under such conditions. The work was broadcast in a studio performance shortly afterwards but was not heard in public until January 1971, in Vienna.

The conservative musical establishment in Germany was appalled by the scandal, especially at Henze's apparent condoning of the students' cause. At once the former darling of the operatic scene was subjected to a form of ostracism; commissions dried up and he was made to feel a pariah. In an interview for a television documentary over two decades later, the pain of that rejection was still audible:

Most of my friends, or my former friends up until then, they dropped me. And [long pause] they dropped me so [long pause] well, they dropped me. There was a moment of quite tremendous isolation, really.

Henze worked out his frustration and anger in a twenty-minute outburst for speaker and orchestra, *Versuch über Schweine* ('Essay on Pigs'), first heard at a London Sinfonietta concert the following February. As music it is a crude and discomfiting experience, a testament to the composer's deep hurt.

One of the ironies of the *Medusa* affair is that the music was totally overlooked. Henze wanted to write revolutionary music to match his revolutionary subject. There is a rawness of tone and an aggressive spirit that make *Das Floss der »Medusa«* an uncomfortable but compelling work to hear. Henze's politicization did not entail a negation of his abilities as a composer; indeed in this and in succeeding works over the next few years the full range of his compositional resources were brought to bear. Side-by-side with the rasping textures in the oratorio are passages of soaring lyricism for the voices, clearly relating to Henze's Italianate music of the 1950s and early 1960s. What did change in his style was the excision of the Stravinskian rhythms present in much of his orchestral output. What replaced it was a burlesque element, often employing popular dance forms. These had crept into his last collaboration with Auden, *Moralities*, in 1967, and were to be elaborated slowly to reach fruition in the political context of the extended song cycle *Voices* in 1973.

Henze further enraged the establishment by making highly publicized visits to Cuba in 1969–70. He wanted to see for himself the revolution in practice and:

... to find out what revolutionary music meant. There was always this discussion going on, the revolution and revolutionary music. What is revolutionary music? And then names would come of people who had a revolutionary way of thinking – politically, sociologically, philosophically. Avant-garde music is not identical with revolutionary thinking. Schoenberg's new system was a bourgeois changing, adding something rather important to the art of composition and the use of the notes of the tempered system; but politically, Schoenberg, Hindemith, Stravinsky – all very right-wing.

In all, Henze spent about twelve months in Cuba, split over two visits. The musical legacy of his time there is by no means slight, embracing major works on a large scale. The first of these was his Sixth Symphony, intended as an 'affirmation, direct avowal of revolution'. Despite its superficially episodic construction, incorporating fragments of revolutionary songs, No. 6 is an impressively achieved three-movement symphony in the grand manner. Henze wanted to turn the great form of Western art-music in on itself but was only partly successful as the work has a musical integrity independent of the radical objective. Quite what the soldiers and farm workers who comprised its first audience made of this complex and intense European work remains unrecorded. In the viola concerto, *Compases para preguntas ensimismadas* ('Questions Asked of One's Soul', 1969–70) and especially in *El Cimarrón*, Henze worked out a more coherent balance of form and content. *El Cimarrón* was designed as a touring, non-staged theatre piece for a singer, flautist, guitarist and percussionist, who all overlap and double-up on various instruments. The text was written by another left-wing German, Hans Magnus Enzensberger, and was based on the life of Esteban Montejo, a runaway slave who had ended up in 1959 a member of Castro's victorious army. During the composition Henze met the now aged Montejo, hearing his experiences at first hand. *El Cimarrón* has achieved classic status in contemporary music. A second project with Enzensberger, the vaudeville *La Cubana, oder Ein Leben für die Kunst* ('The Cuban Woman, or a Life for the Arts'), based on the life of a cabaret singer, has failed to establish itself in the repertoire.

Che Guevara, Communist revolutionary and dedicatee of Henze's oratorio *The Raft of the 'Medusa'*

Back in Europe, Henze applied his newly intensified motivation to a string of works which in varying ways broke the bounds of the mediums they employed. The Second Violin Concerto is a case in point, a half-hour-long cantata for solo violin (the player being obliged to recite a poem by Enzensberger during the performance), baritone and orchestra. The solo violinist is also required to wear a florid, harlequin-like costume whilst playing. Another theatre piece, but like *El Cimarrón* and *La Cubana* not truly operatic, appeared in 1971: *Der langwierige Weg in die Wohnung der Natascha Ungeheuer* ('The Tedious Way to the Place of Natascha Frightful'), the Berlin première of which was hissed and booed as heartily as *Der junge Lord* had been acclaimed only six years earlier. Henze's symphonic poem *Heliogabalus Imperator* (subtitled 'Allegory for Music' and named after one of the less well-known insane emperors of the third-century Roman Empire) was completed in 1972 and first conducted by Sir Georg Solti with the Chicago Symphony Orchestra on 16 November that year.

The composition of *Voices* signalled the high-water mark in the first phase of Henze's music of political commitment. It also occasioned a synthesis of the many disparate new strands in his output since his embracing of a more radical cause six years before. Whereas in *The Bassarids* he had successfully fused a powerful language expressed in a single accent, *Voices* gloried in its diversity. Here all types of popular, almost folk, elements from different countries were combined in a sprawling series of twenty-two songs on subjects including imprisonment, murder and the nature of art. Two singers – one male, one female – are accompanied by a large chamber ensemble which includes such instruments as steel drum, ocarina, banjo, electric guitar and accordion. The texts also represent a wide and eclectic range, Enzensberger rubbing shoulders with Brecht, Ho Chi Minh and several Cuban writers. *Voices* was again premièred in London, on 4 January 1974, by the mezzo-soprano Rose Taylor and tenor Paul Sperry. The composer himself conducted the London Sinfonietta, cementing the relationship with the ensemble and its audience begun a few years earlier under the aegis of its co-founder Michael Vyner, a long-standing friend of Henze.

Whilst in London in 1972, Henze had spent some time experimenting with taped sounds. Ostensibly, this was to create the pre-recorded tape required in the Second Violin Concerto, then still awaiting its first performance. It gave him the opportunity to develop certain ideas beginning to form for another large-scale instrumental piece. This turned out eventually to be a third piano concerto in the form of six preludes for piano, tape and orchestra: *Tristan*. This work is a many-layered musical exploration of facets of the myriad stories enveloping the mythical character of the medieval knight of German romance. The tragedy of Tristan and Isolde, the climax of Henze's piece, became counterpointed by other calamities in his own life. At one point the choreographer John Cranko was interested in creating a ballet on the same legends using Henze's music, but Cranko died before any concrete plan could materialize. In September 1973, the radical left-wing movement in Europe was appalled by the military coup of General Pinochet in Chile, which overthrew the first freely elected Marxist government and murdered its leader, Salvador Allende. Refugees flocked to Europe, many staying close to Henze's home in Marino. They recounted horrific tales of the torture and murder of anyone felt to be an opponent of the military regime, the book burnings recalling Nazi terror and oppression. In that same month, two of Henze's former collaborators, Auden and Ingeborg Bachmann, both died – the latter in a fire. *Tristan* became a memorial to those events.

The more obviously personal stamp of *Tristan*, the first work of any size since 1967 that was personal or primarily musical in motivation, allowed Henze to broaden the range of music that he employed in his more political output. In 1974 he teamed up with Edward Bond, the left-wing British playwright, to create an opera. *We come to the River* occupies a special place amongst his works for the stage. It is a music drama on an enormous scale (Bond's description was 'actions for music') and is split across three separate semi-stages. Instruments and characters become identified with each other and with particular areas of the stage. Henze regards it as his 'best opera'. Working with Bond was a convivial experience and, like Auden, the British writer had definite ideas for the musical character of the opera. In *We come to the River*, Henze took up again the central theme of most of his earlier stage works. The central figure is an unnamed general who, having suppressed a rebellion against the emperor, is forced to face the prospect of his impending blindness. Paradoxically, his vision

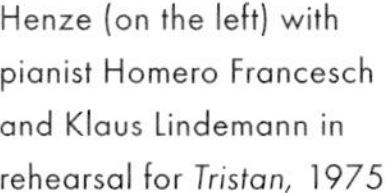

Henze (on the left) with pianist Homero Francesch and Klaus Lindemann in rehearsal for *Tristan*, 1975

becomes keener and the painful realization dawns on him of the suffering his actions have brought down on others. His self-examination leads him to fall foul of the provincial governor who has the general placed in an asylum. In this work, more than in any of the others, Henze came closest to the fundamental question lying at the heart of Hindemith's three great operas (*Cardillac, Mathis der Maler* and *Die Harmonie der Welt*), albeit from a militarist rather than artistic angle, and Hartmann's *Simplicius Simplicissimus. We come to the River* is in large part a continuation of these forebears. The general, if not an artist, is a near relative – war being his art, the maintenance of the state his raison d'être, which events betray.

We come to the River received its world première at the Royal Opera House, Covent Garden, on 12 July 1976. Henze produced the opera himself, assisted by David Pountney, and Henze's youngest brother, Jürgen, designed the scenery and costumes. In the programme booklet, Bond and Henze jointly published a statement concerning the political nature of art:

> *Men without politics would be animals and art without politics would be trivial ... Art isn't involved in itself. If there are H-bombs and concentration camps art either acknowledges this (and makes these things its subject, literally or analytically) or it deliberately turns its back on them and so falsifies reality. It can't turn aside and pursue its own path, it has no path. Art is realism or it is trivial, and there's nothing much in between. We could rewrite the parable of the man who fell among thieves: an artist came down the road, saw the wounded men in the gutter, crossed over to pass by on the other side, and fell in a ditch and broke his neck.*

The opera played to empty houses and critical indifference. Henze was never invited back to Covent Garden.

During the composition of the opera, Henze turned again to writing purely instrumental chamber music on a scale unparalleled in his output since before his flight to Italy. Starting with a short Trio for Mandolin, Guitar and Harp, written in 1974 as film music for Granada Television in Manchester, Henze proceeded to compose over the next dozen years well over two dozen works for a wide range of instruments. These included ensemble pieces for winds and strings such as *Amicizia* ('Friendship', 1976), *L'Autunno* ('Autumn', 1977), *Canzona* (1982) and the Sonata for Six Players (1984) as well as solo pieces for guitar (the two sonatas on Shakespearean characters *Royal Winter Music* in 1976 and 1979), violin, double bass, marimba, viola, cello and piano. At the centre of this activity was a set of three strings quartets (Nos. 3, 4 and 5), commissioned by the Schwetzingen festival, and begun before work on the opera was finished. The composition of quartets in groups has been extremely rare in the twentieth century, although it was a commonplace in the eighteenth, as the output of Haydn, Mozart and Beethoven amongst others all attest. Even Hindemith had produced his quartets singly, unlike his sonatas. Henze's Third, Fourth and Fifth Quartets all derive much of their musical material from *We come to the River* and share memorial inspirations, respectively occasioned by Henze's mother (who died on New Year's Night, 1976), Victor Jara (who like the poet, Pablo Neruda, died as a consequence of the Pinochet coup) and the composer Benjamin Britten. The three works are quite unlike each other in size and profile. The Third is a radiant elegy in a single twenty-minute span, while the Fourth is nearly twice as long in four separate movements (its second movement alone runs to a quarter of an hour in duration and contains the profoundest music of all of his quartets). The exploratory Fifth incorporates elements of both immediate predecessors in its six brief movements.

Three of the instrumental works of the mid to late 1970s, a Sonatina for Violin and Piano, a set of six pieces for piano, and three *Märchenbilder* for guitar, were extracted from his children's opera *Pollicino*. This work was written in 1979–80 for a very different audience. Henze had in 1975 become involved with a local festival in the small Tuscan town of Montepulciano. Using only the local populace and their brass band, he instigated a thriving festival, one of its specialities being modern realizations of operas from earlier centuries. Concerts were also a regular feature and very soon music students and professional groups became attracted to the workshops or *cantieri*, as they were called. The first involved a group of more-or-less advanced composers – including Peter Maxwell Davies – working on a collective composition, the opera *Der Ofen* ('The Furnace'), a protest against the air pollution in large cities. For the second *cantiere*, the first in which local people played an active and dynamic role,

Left, Henze photographed in familiar pose, c. 1989

Henze turned to the comic opera *Don Chisciotte della Mancia* ('Don Quixote from La Mancha') by Giovanni Paisiello. Henze's interest in and adaptation of older music was nothing new; in 1976 he had already made his own performing version of the oratorio *Jephte* by Giacomo Carissimi. Henze and librettist Giuseppe Di Leva completely updated the plot of Cervantes' ancient knight, creating a more 'politically aware' version of the Don Quixote story, adding enough new scenes and music for the result to be classified as a new work altogether. One of the most vital aspects of the Montepulciano *cantieri* was the empowerment of the local people, not just as audience, but as performers and producers. Local schoolchildren translated into Italian the libretto of *Pollicino* which London schoolchildren had compiled from stories by Collodi, Grimm and Perrault under the guidance of Edward Bond; Di Leva and Henze then wove an opera for the Tuscan children to present themselves. Many of the events were thrown together or hastily recast at the last moment, depending on who was to hand. On one early occasion a travelling mime group who arrived unexpectedly were thrown on stage to act out Rossini's *Il turco in Italia* ('The Turk in Italy'). A later, locally designed production of Stravinsky's *The Soldier's Tale* as street-theatre was toured to local villages.

Even at Montepulciano, politics – albeit of decidedly local demeanour – intruded. One rather vocal section of the inhabitants were committed opponents of the festivals, primarily on account of the expense. The presence of Henze and other left-wing sympathizers fuelled the resentment of these conservative dissenters and led to the cancellation of one performance in the 1976 *cantiere*. The squabble was occasioned by a request for travelling expenses for the mime group which the mayor refused. As the years passed, however, the *cantiere*, by involving more and more of the local people and attracting more business to the town, slowly began to circumvent this hostility.

Away from Tuscany, Henze's collaboration with Bond continued with the idea – or rather an obsession – of a work based on the subject of Orpheus. It started with a lecture given at the eventful 1976 *cantiere* by the scholar Franco Serpa. Bond was at first unsure; as Henze later wrote to Josef Rufer in 1979: 'I spent a whole afternoon walking up and down in his study, trying to answer his question *why* I wanted to write an Orpheus. By the end of the visit I still had not managed to explain it clearly, for I myself did not know; I know only my musical reasons and desires connected with the theme in question.' Formative influences of these desires included a particularly vivid account of the seventeenth-century opera *Orfeo* by Claudio Monteverdi. In the same letter to Rufer, Henze identified the precise moment when he knew he wanted to compose an Orpheus of his own:

> *It was while I was packing my case after having conducted* Heliogabalus Imperator *in the Amsterdam Concertgebouw. A heron was sitting on a post in the misty Amstel. The previous evening at a party I had met an unusually feminine creature, reddish and mask-like, motherly like everything seductive, like Eurydice, who reigns over a wide territory that was then still unknown to me, the goddess of the dead, the dead goddess.*

An integral part of Henze's conception was that this would be a ballet, his first since *Tancredi* in 1964, and not an opera. The recent instrumental works that he had been writing facilitated this non-vocal approach; indeed Henze described the three Quartets for Schwetzingen and the Solo Violin Sonata (1976) as works '*en route* to the Orpheus music'. So indeed was the first *Royal Winter Music* sonata for guitar (as a modern equivalent of Orpheus's lyre) and two sets of orchestral variations. The ballet is another synthesizing work in Henze's output, particularly of the music of commitment. As with *Don Chisciotte della Mancia*, the ancient myth was updated from an avowedly political standpoint – the Olympian gods appearing as oppressors while the dead in Hades became equated with 'all those who suffer'. Orpheus's attempt to lead Eurydice out of the kingdom of the dead took on an additional, almost revolutionary significance.

Henze's *Orpheus* was first presented in Stuttgart on 17 March 1979, but like *König Hirsch* subsequently came to exist in multiple versions. Almost immediately on its completion Henze prepared a concert work of ninety minutes' duration for speaker and orchestra, whilst after the première two sets of 'dramatic scenes' were extracted from the body of the score. A set of instrumental *Arien des Orpheus* ('Songs of Orpheus') for guitar, harp, harpsichord and strings and a *Toccata senza Fuga* ('Toccata without Fugue') for organ were also turned into

Henze in rehearsal for a television performance of *Barcarola*, with conductor Gerd Albrecht in 1987

separate concert items. In 1986, Henze prepared a new version of the ballet which enjoyed a triumphantly successful run in Vienna. The direction and choreography were by Ruth Berghaus, 'a director who as a young person was a dancer and choreographer ... it was very impressive, a huge success, sold-out houses whenever they put it on. That was quite extraordinary, a theatrical director who was also a choreographer.' The ballet had a further spin-off: for the original Stuttgart première, Bond penned some poems in place of a note for the programme book. In 1981–3, Henze set these for unaccompanied chorus under the title *Orpheus behind the Wire*, producing one of the classic twentieth-century repertoire items in the process.

Henze's final venture with Edward Bond was *The English Cat*. Work on this satirical opera occupied the composer on and off for four years from 1978, during which he kept a journal, published in 1983. The entries recorded both personal details and aspects of this and other compositions. Bond took a short story by Honoré de Balzac as the starting point for this anthropomorphic tale of aristocratic late-Victorian cats and their passion for money. Henze constructed his score to resemble an eighteenth- or early nineteenth-century opera. Archaic musical forms abound, such as the courante,

Above, a scene from *The English Cat*, in a production at Nuremberg 1986
Right, a performance of *Der junge Lord* by the Komische Oper Berlin, 1968

terzetto, recitative and quodlibet, although more modern elements appear in the number 'Collages' and a tango. Like *The Bassarids*, *The English Cat* was first performed in a German translation, as with *Orpheus* in Stuttgart, on 2 June 1983, conducted by Dennis Russell Davies. Since that time it has been successfully staged many times in Germany as well as in the USA, France, Britain and Italy (at Bologna and also at a Montepulciano *cantiere*).

Henze returned to purely orchestral composition in 1979, with *Barcarola*. That year, Henze's staunch friend and long-standing comrade-in-arms Paul Dessau had died and *Barcarola* was dedicated to his memory. The barcarole as a musical form originated as a gondolier's song, but in the nineteenth century became more widely appreciated in an instrumental guise, particularly in the hands of the Polish composer–pianist, Frédéric Chopin. Henze's gondolier in *Barcarola* was Charon, the ferryman of Greek myth who transported the dead across the river Styx. Perhaps because of the personal nature of the dedication, *Barcarola* is written in a more traditional style than much of his mature music, with a greater reliance on tonality. His next orchestral piece was on a much larger scale though also imbued in part by a memorial air. The composer outlined its structure for a recording in 1993:

My Seventh Symphony is a German symphony and it deals with matters German. The first part is an Allemande – a German dance that gains increasing force and energy ... The second ... is relatively straightforward: I see it as a kind of funeral ode, a song of lamentation, a monologue. The third ... is cast in the form of a scherzo ... While writing it I thought of the sufferings of Friedrich Hölderlin immured in the Authenried Asylum in Tübingen, where the treatment he received ... amounted to nothing short of the most terrible torture. The final section is ... an orchestral setting of Hölderlin's late poem Hälfte des Lebens *['Half of Life'].*

Following page, re-unification in sight, 31 January 1989: East Germans stand atop the Wall, politically breached but not yet demolished

The symphony was composed to commission from the Berlin Philharmonic Orchestra and given its première by them under Gianluigi Gelmetti on 1 December 1984. The symphony was the clearest crystallization thus far of a wish to return to his cultural roots. This has found expression in his vocal music as well, as he explains:

Now in his late sixties, Henze (seen here with the conductor Claudio Abbado at a concert in the *Wien modern* 92 series) is fêted internationally by artists and music festivals.

I would like to set more in my mother tongue because I understand it better [Henze has an impressive command of several languages other than German and Italian, not least English and Spanish]. I did Auden three times and Bond three times in English, Pollicino *in Italian and now I feel the vibrations of the word, of the phrase, the thing that makes me respond to it musically. I can do best when I know exactly and profoundly what the meaning is, without a shadow of doubt.*

The most impressive monument to this desire that has been achieved to date is Henze's fourteenth opera, *Das verratene Meer* ('The Betrayed Sea', 1986–9). The libretto, by Hans-Ulrich Treichel, is based on the story *The Sailor who Fell from Grace with the Sea* by the Japanese writer Yukio Mishima. *Das verratene Meer* received its world première conducted by Markus Stenz at the Deutsche Oper in Berlin on 5 May 1990, almost six months to the day after the breaching of the Berlin Wall.

A rapprochement with German culture uncoloured by political conviction manifested itself in many other ways including the orchestral scores from the 1980s, the Seventh Symphony being an obvious example. Others included *I sentimenti di Carl Philipp Emanuel Bach*, a set of transcriptions for flute, harp and strings of music by that composer from 1787, and *An eine Äolsharfe* ('To an Aeolian Harp') for guitar and chamber ensemble which drew on poems by Mörike for inspiration. On a more practical level, Henze became involved with a summer academy named after him run each year in his home town of Gütersloh and was appointed in 1988 as artistic director of the Munich Biennial festival where he commissioned important new operas by the young British composers Mark-Anthony Turnage and Benedict Mason. For this he maintains a flat in the Bavarian capital but has no desire to return to live in his country of birth. 'The thing is, living in Italy I live as an Italian, I pay my tax in Italy but I also speak the language. I'm with Italians from morning to night – that's my daily life.' Henze's partner of thirty years, Fausto Moroni, is from Calabria in southern Italy. 'I think and act in Italian and ... there have been times when I wanted to become Italian.' As if to reinforce the cosmopolitan point, Henze has allowed his gaze to move to several other countries for inspiration, not least Great Britain. The seven instrumental *Liebeslieder* ('Love-songs') of 1984–5, a cello concerto in all but name, derived its form and content from various English poems (the identity of which Henze has not disclosed) in a manner not unlike that of *An eine Äolsharfe*.

The composition of the nine spiritual concertos for piano, trumpet and large chamber orchestra that collectively form the *Requiem* was inaugurated by the untimely death in 1989 of Michael Vyner, the London Sinfonietta's artistic director. Over the next three years Henze slowly constructed this enormous and elaborate score; the individual component movements or concertos, which can be grouped into subsets of the nine, were first performed individually at various times from 1990 onwards, the whole only being heard together for the first time in February 1993. The titles, taken from the Catholic Mass for the Dead, are 'metaphors for concepts or states of imagination like fear, mourning, pain, catastrophe, oppression, panic, loneliness, loss ... The titles should thus be seen as doors through which one can pass, in order to find the new, non-liturgical, personal expression and shape of the work.' Any notion that the work drew on or reflected the contemporaneous political revolutions in Eastern Europe, the demolition of the Berlin Wall or reunification of Germany are firmly denied by the composer: 'I reject this interpretation wholeheartedly. The *Requiem* is a personal piece.' The Piano Quintet (1990–91) shares some of the *Requiem*'s hardness of sound. As with the Seventh Symphony, it is avowedly about 'matters German', in this case purely musical ones, particularly the composer's 'experience of nineteenth-century classical techniques' as found in Beethoven and Brahms.

Henze's Eighth Symphony is overtly programmatic, taking its inspiration from three episodes in Shakespeare's *A Midsummer Night's Dream*. Composed during 1992–3, the first movement is based on the passage in the play …

where Oberon describes to Puck how he has to travel to get that magic flower and I composed a description of this trip in which the climax is when Cupid shoots his arrow into the centre of the moon. Then Puck says 'I'll put a girdle round the world in forty minutes' – I take only seven! … The second movement is the two love scenes between Bottom and Titania … we don't know exactly what happened between them … the music might tell us and give an idea. And the last one is a kind of epilogue with Puck saying 'If we shadows have offended …'; his last goodbye to the audience, apologizing.

The symphony was first performed in Boston under the direction of Seiji Ozawa on 1 October 1993. There seems no danger yet of Henze bidding a last goodbye, and he is currently busy with a new operatic project. The works of Shakespeare, which made a great impression on him when he was still a student during the 1940s, have lately proved a fecund source of inspiration, as the *Royal Winter Music* and Eighth Symphony show. The initial impetus for *Der junge Lord* in 1964 was for an adaptation of *Love's Labour's Lost*, but Ingeborg Bachmann was not keen. Since then, Henze has nurtured an ambition for a Shakespearean stage work and will achieve this with *Venus and Adonis*, freely adapted from the Bard's poem by Hans-Ulrich Treichel. The work is to be staged in 1996 by the Munich State Opera to mark the composer's seventieth birthday.

Epilogue

The role of German music in the twentieth century cannot be overestimated. It has been a tale of domination and retreat, experiment and control, research and systematization that has mirrored the political and military fortunes that the nation has endured. There is probably no area of Western music that has not been touched by the Expressionist and atonal movements that arose around the time of the First World War or serialism after the Second. Yet for the period of the Third Reich such experiment was erased from the country, along with many of the leading traditional composers. No discussion of German music in the 1930s and 1940s can be complete without at least a mention of the artistic ghetto that flourished in the Nazi controlled environment of the walled town of Theresienstadt (modern Terezín), a waystation to the death camps at Auschwitz-Birkenau. The inhabitants may not have been German – most were of Czech origin, though some German–Jewish composers, artists and musicians were present – but the compositions produced there under appalling conditions were German in orientation, politically if not musically.

Hindemith, Hartmann and Henze were all involved with radicalism in both the musical and political arenas. All three indulged in experiments early in their careers and helped to foster the continued development of new music by others. In the event, all of them moved away from a pioneer stance, tending to avoid the dictates of schools or cliques. Ultimately, their musical roots are intertwined and spring from the mainstream tradition of German music. There is an audible progression from the music of Bruckner, Reger and Richard Strauss through Hindemith's, Hartmann's and Henze's works. In the second half of the twentieth century this tradition became sidelined by the more media-conscious experimenters who adhered to an alternative progression from the music of Mahler and the new Viennese school of, principally, Schoenberg and Webern. Henze and, to a lesser degree, Hartmann, were both flexible enough to take advantage of both areas of activity; Hindemith remained more conservatively faithful to the old ways with a backward-looking but still vital method. Hartmann and Henze both learned much from Hindemith's music, particularly that of the 1920s. Hindemith and Hartmann both exercised a direct influence on Henze.

Henze was influenced in many ways, not just musically, by Hartmann. 'Whenever I came to see him,' Henze recalls, 'he was so kind to show me what he was doing. The score was always there on the piano or the huge desk he had made there.' These visits turned out to be 'the only lessons in orchestration that I have ever had from anybody ... about mixing colours and the refinement of it and the wonderful writing – the scores were always magnificent. That impressed me a lot and encouraged me to try to be as meticulous in the notation; it should look beautiful graphically. There is a kind of satisfaction for a composer to make something graphically attractive in the score. It is part of the aesthetic, creative satisfaction.' Hartmann's personal integrity also profoundly moved the young composer. 'There was something that was a novelty for me; Fortner didn't have this, nobody really – Leibowitz by then I had worked with and he didn't have it either – this ardent concern for people and their fate; and with the drama of the Germans falling into the hands of the Nazis. He was really an ardent anti-Fascist and an ardent, modern man concerned with the question of equality, respect for others in the sense of Rosa Luxemburg who said: "Freedom lies in the freedom of one who thinks differently."' The orchestral arrangement made in 1995 by Henze of Hartmann's Piano Sonata '27 April 1945' clearly has connotations extending far beyond the purely musical.

At various times in their careers Hindemith, Hartmann and Henze were not permitted the luxury of thinking differently in Germany, yet still managed to pursue their artistic vision by recourse to exile, either internal or external. Despite their links being severed with the day-to-day musical life of the country at differing times, their collective output has in a very real sense preserved and revitalized the traditional forms of sonata, concerto, symphony and opera. But Hindemith's refusal to return to his homeland was symptomatic of the attitude of many refugees after 1945, and thus Germany never recovered her pre-war eminence. Another important and positive facet of the work of all three is that between them their music, however uniformly secular in aesthetic, reconciled the historic division of

German culture between the Protestant north and Catholic south. This resolution was occasioned by political unity and their individual family backgrounds. The reconciliation of at times hostile elements became particularly pertinent given the political unifications and divisions of recent German history – the main thrust of which has been towards the creation of a single nation. Collectively, their works can be seen as a fixed point around which the bewildering diversity of post-war German music, ranging from the proto-minimalism of Orff to the experimental extremes of Stockhausen, has revolved. Hindemith, Hartmann and Henze are arguably the three finest composers to have emerged from Germany in the past hundred years, endowing their country with music of exceptional quality as well as a continuity of expression and intent of incalculable importance for the fractured history of German culture – and indeed the nation itself – this century.

The individual legacies of these three composers are, however, highly varied. Hindemith will be remembered chiefly for the opera *Mathis der Maler* and the symphony culled from it, along with a handful of genuinely popular orchestral works, such as the *Symphonic Metamorphoses on Themes of Weber* and several solo concertos. The bulk of actual performances has derived, however, from the series of instrumental sonatas. His crucial work as a teacher and theorist should not be underestimated and was international in scope. The publication of his educational theories spread his influence still wider for a short time before being overtaken by the serialist demagogues of the Darmstadt summer school. Hartmann's legacy likewise extends beyond his composed music, the Musica Viva concerts in particular enjoying international prestige, being replicated elsewhere in Germany, Europe and the USA. As a composer, Hartmann's work was overlooked for decades outside of Bavaria, but the chamber opera *Simplicius Simplicissimus* and eight numbered symphonies are vital compositions in the recent development of central European music and are the works upon which Hartmann's reputation rests and is starting to spread. By contrast, Henze spent the best part of three decades playing hide-and-seek with many of the traditional forms and conventions of German music. This is partly explained by his rejection of his homeland and can be heard in the Italianate ethos of much of his output. In his later symphonies a more genuinely symphonic attitude has been promulgated, consciously evoking comparison with the works of his nineteenth-century forebears, although in No. 6 this was mainly for political purposes. Henze's principal legacy lies with his operas rather than his instrumental music, however important individual quartets, symphonies or works such as the *Requiem* or the Piano Quintet (1990–91) may appear to be.

When Hindemith died in 1963, his life's work was substantively complete. Hartmann died too young and this loss must be counted amongst the greatest in modern peacetime Germany. Henze as a composer is still developing new ideas although the music of his seventh decade bears signs of greater stylistic unity. In the later symphonies, Henze has taken up Hartmann's mantle in tackling the problems of large-scale musical construction. Though in No. 7 Henze does not advance beyond Hartmann's achievement, in No. 8 he at least opens up the direction for his twenty-first-century successors to follow. One will look in vain for a single work of synthesis in his output to stand with *Mathis der Maler* or *Die Harmonie der Welt* in Hindemith's. At various points along the path of his career, Henze has produced compositions which can stand as exemplars of the salient points of his style at a given time: *The Bassarids* and *Orpheus* are two such works. The diversity of his music, however, has precluded any all-encompassing single masterpiece; rather, as with the songs of *Voices*, it is the variety and disparity in his works that is the point.

The symphony has tended to dominate the orchestral output of each composer (although less centrally in Hindemith's case) and to provide a common thread running through their compositional careers. Between them – up until 1993 – they produced twenty-four such works (if one includes Hartmann's *Sinfonia tragica* and *Klagegesang*). Comparisons of their instrumental and chamber output reveal a less uniform situation, although no less representative of each one's respective artistic preoccupations. Hindemith was perhaps the instrumental composer *par excellence*: a virtuoso on both the violin and viola as well as technically of concert rank on the piano and clarinet, he possessed an innate practical musicality that allowed him to acquire a working knowledge of almost every standard (and several definitely non-standard) instruments, something he tended to demand, unreasonably or not, from his composition students. He was a man who seemed to live and breathe music and his ever-inquisitive mind led him to examine and write for many unusual and exotic species. Including his mature chamber works, which with the solo pieces run to well in excess of one hundred separate items, Hindemith covered practically every major instrumental combination. By contrast, Hartmann's contribution to chamber music appears sparse almost to the point of parsimony, especially when viewing his mature output. Of the sixteen pieces that he composed for solo instruments or chamber groups only three date from after 1933: the Second Piano Sonata '27 April 1945', the Second String Quartet and the unfinished Scherzo for percussion ensemble. Once Hartmann began to tackle orchestral composition during the last months of 1933 he rarely went back to chamber music, unlike Hindemith for whom it was a lifelong interest. As with Hartmann, Henze's instrumental and chamber works are spread unevenly across his five decades of mature composition. In the late 1940s, still inexperienced, Henze produced instrumental sonatas for a number of instruments along with two string quartets. Between 1952, the year Henze completed his Quartet No. 2 and a Wind Quintet, and the mid-1970s, when he returned to the smaller abstract forms with a vengeance, there are perhaps half-a-dozen solo or ensemble pieces. None of them is of equivalent importance to those of Hindemith's sonatas or quartets or Henze's own orchestral, vocal and operatic output of the time; indeed most were written as satellite studies to larger undertakings. From 1974, Henze returned to chamber composition, with the set of three string quartets connected to *We come to the River*.

Given his strong desire to communicate directly and vitally with an audience, it is not surprising that music for the voice figures so prominently in Henze's catalogue, bringing to mind the similar disposition of Benjamin Britten. Indeed, vocal music, whether operatic or in concert, has remained the most apparent manifestation of Henze's art, in the way that the sonata came to represent Hindemith or the symphony Hartmann. The militant protest phase that Henze sustained after 1967 is most immediately encountered in his vocal works, which were designed to shock and provoke audiences much as Hindemith's more extreme pieces of the 1920s were. Hindemith may not have been at all political in his approach but his radicalism was accelerated by the revolutionary ferment following the Great War. What is also not often appreciated is the extent and range of

Hindemith's vocal music; several of his operas may be well enough known, but the voice figured in his compositions all through his life, from songs written in his student days before World War I through song-cycles, oratorios and motets to the fine unaccompanied Mass completed in his last year. As befits Hartmann's sparing productivity, there are only a handful of works involving voices, but all of them are major items.

If the symphonies were produced in sufficient numbers to allow meaningful parallels between the three composers, this is not the case with their music for the stage. Hindemith produced seven operas and two ballets in the 1920s, but after *Mathis der Maler* was finally staged in 1938 wrote only two further operas – *Die Harmonie der Welt* alone being a full-scale piece – and three short ballets. There is little doubt that the flame of theatrical composition, which had been of inestimable importance for him early on, in general burned low from the late 1930s. Hartmann is the odd one out in having undertaken just two operatic ventures (both pre-Second World War) and no ballets, in marked contrast to Henze's consistent cultivation of music for the theatre throughout his life. So far, not counting the not-yet-complete *Venus and Adonis*, Henze has created fourteen operas, twelve ballets or pantomimes and four other stage works (such as *La Cubana* from 1973), outstripping both Hindemith and Hartmann together in quantity.

If all three composers are increasingly seen, with the passage of time, as being amongst the most important of the twentieth century in Germany, their relevance and achievement also has a wider aspect. Hindemith, by entering the standard repertoire, rooted in the Classical and Romantic periods with a few truly popular works, has attained a status analogous to those twentieth-century composers like Prokofiev, Shostakovich and Stravinsky, who have found a different audience neither concerned by, nor versed in, the conventions of art music. If *Mathis der Maler* cannot be compared in terms of public appeal to *Peter and the Wolf* or *The Rite of Spring*, it has none the less become a staple of the modern orchestral repertoire. Neither Hartmann nor Henze has enjoyed such success, but Henze's stature amongst the smaller and more informed audience of contemporary music is by far the greatest of the three. Hartmann in many respects falls between the two, neither as traditionally based nor as popular in appeal as Hindemith (the music is perhaps too aggressive for that) nor as consciously revolutionary and innovative in intent as Henze. And yet, it is in Hartmann's works, particularly the symphonies, that the essence of the German tradition has been most consistently and effectively maintained. In musical terms, the answer to the German Question of the twenty-first century will reveal how Hartmann's legacy comes to be applied.

Classified List of Works

The lists which follow (ordered alphabetically by composer) are based primarily on the current catalogues of Hindemith, Hartmann and Henze and other documentation of their common publisher, now Schott Musik International of Mainz. Additional unpublished works are constantly coming to light, for Hindemith and Hartmann especially, so these lists cannot claim to be wholly definitive, but are as complete as possible at the time of going to press. Arrangements of their works by other composers have been omitted. Details of first performances, particularly during the Nazi period, are also unavailable for several works; where they cannot be confirmed absolutely I have marked them 'fp?'.

Karl Amadeus Hartmann

In his autobiographical writings Hartmann stated that he destroyed much of his earliest music and apprentice pieces from the 1920s and 1930s. These works are not listed and there are few surviving indications as to their character or instrumentation. Other later projects that Hartmann considered and planned are also omitted unless a substantial fragment is known to have been extant at some time.

Works are listed according to the following categories: Opera, Orchestral, Solo Instrument(s) with Orchestra, Chamber/Instrumental, Choral, Vocal.

Opera

Wachsfigurenkabinett ('Wax Dolls' Display Case'): Five short operas (1929–30; unfinished), librettos by Erich Bormann. fp Munich, 29 May 1988

Das Leben und Sterben des heiligen Teufels ('The Life and Death of the Holy Devil')

Der Mann, der vom Tode auferstand ('The Man, Who Rose from the Dead'), completed by Günter Bialas and Henze

Chaplin–Ford–Trott: Scenic Jazz Cantata, completed by Wilfried Hiller

Fürwahr?! ('Really?!'), completed by Henze

Die Witwe von Ephesus ('The Widow of Ephesus')

Simplicius Simplicissimus, original title *Des Simplicius Simplicissimus Jugend* ('The Youth of Simplicius Simplicissimus'). Libretto by Hermann Scherchen, Wolfgang Petzet and the composer after Hans Jakob von Grimmelshausen (1934–5). fp (concert) Munich, 2 April 1948; (stage) Cologne, 20 October 1949. Revised version, 1956–7. fp (stage) Mannheim, 9 July 1957

Orchestral

Symphonic Poem: *Miserae* (1933–4). fp Prague, 2 September 1935

Suite from the opera: *Simplicius Simplicissimus*, for small orchestra (1934–5). fp?

Symphony No. 1 (also *Symphonic Fragments*), *Versuch eines Requiems* ('Essay towards a Requiem'), for alto and orchestra, text: Walt Whitman (1935–6, revised 1954–5). fp Vienna, 22 June 1957

Symphony: *L'Oeuvre*, after Emile Zola (1937–8). fp Liège, Belgium, July 1939. Rewritten in 1951–3 as Symphony No. 6

Symphony (also *Symphonic Concerto*), for string orchestra and soprano, text by Kong Fu-Tse, translated by Klabund (1938). Unperformed. Rewritten in 1947–8 as Symphony No. 4

Incidental Music for Shakespeare's *Macbeth* (*c.* 1940, unfinished). Unperformed

Sinfonia tragica (1940, revised 1943). fp Munich, 20 May 1989. (First movement re-used in 1948–9 as finale of Symphony No. 3)

Symphoniae dramaticae:

Symphonic Overture (originally titled *China kämpft*, 'China Struggles', 1942). fp Darmstadt, 26 July 1947. Revised version, 1962. fp Nuremberg, 28 November 1975

Symphonic Hymns, for large orchestra (1941–3). fp Munich, 9 October 1975

Symphonic Suite: *Vita Nova* ('New Life'), for reciter and orchestra (1941–2, unfinished?). Unperformed

Adagio for large orchestra: Symphony No. 2 (?1940–4, revised 1946). fp Donaueschingen, 10 September 1950

Symphony: *Klagegesang* ('Hymn of Lamentation'; also *Symphonic Expressions*, 1944–7). fp Berlin, 16 June 1990. Partly rewritten in 1948–9 as movements I and II of Symphony No. 3

Symphony No. 4, for string orchestra (1947–8, from Symphony for Strings and Soprano, 1938). fp Munich, 2 April 1948

Symphony No. 3 (1948–9, from movements extracted from *Sinfonia tragica*, 1940–3, and *Klagegesang*, 1944–7). fp Munich, 10 February 1950

Symphonie concertante: Symphony No. 5 (1950, from Trumpet Concerto, 1932–3/Concerto for Wind and Double Basses, 1948–9). fp Stuttgart, 21 April 1951

Symphony No. 6 (1951–3, from Symphony *L'Oeuvre*, 1937–8). fp Munich, 24 April 1953

Symphony No. 7 (1957–8). fp Hamburg, 15 March 1959

Symphony No. 8 (1960–62). fp Cologne 25 January 1963

Solo Instrument(s) with Orchestra

Kleines Konzert ('Little Concerto'), for string quartet and percussion (1931–2). fp Munich, September 1932. Version for string orchestra and percussion arranged Henning Brauel. fp Braunschweig, 29 November 1974

Concerto for Wind and Solo Trumpet (1932–3). fp Strasbourg, 1933. Revised in 1948–9 as Concerto for Wind and Double Basses

Cello Concerto (*c.* 1933; lost, probably unfinished). Unperformed

Triple Concerto (also *Symphonie–Divertissement*), for bassoon, tenor trombone, double bass and chamber orchestra (*c.* 1933–4; unfinished,completion by Andrew McCredie in preparation). Unperformed

Kammerkonzert ('Chamber Concerto'), for clarinet, string quartet and string orchestra (1930–5). fp Zürich, 17 June 1969

Concerto funebre (originally *Musik der Trauer*, 'Music of Mourning'), for violin and string orchestra (1939). fp St Gallen, Switzerland, 1940. Revised version, 1959. fp Braunschweig, 12 November 1959

Concerto for Wind and Double Basses (1948–9). fp Zürich, November 1949. Revised in 1950 as Symphony No. 5

Concerto for Piano, Wind and Percussion (1953). fp Donaueschingen, 10 October 1953

Concerto for Viola with Piano, accompanied by wind and percussion (1954–6). fp Frankfurt am Main, 25 May 1956

Chamber/Instrumental

Little Suite No. 1 for Piano (*c.* 1924–6). fp Cologne, 22 November 1989

Little Suite No. 2 for Piano (*c.* 1924–6). fp Cologne, 22 November 1989

Sonata No. 1 for Solo Violin (1927). fp Munich, 28 June 1987

Sonata No. 2 for Solo Violin (1927). fp Munich, 28 June 1987

Suite No. 1 for Solo Violin (1927). fp Spokane, Washington, 6 April 1986

Suite No. 2 for Solo Violin (1927). fp Spokane, Washington, 5 February 1984

Jazz Toccata and Fugue, for piano (1927–8). fp?

Tanzsuite ('Dance Suite'), for clarinet, bassoon, trumpet, horn and trombone (1931). fp Munich, 1931

Burleske Musik, for flute, clarinet, bassoon, horn, trumpet, trombone, percussion and piano (1931). fp Munich, 1931

Piano Sonatina (1931). fp Munich, 4 January 1932

Toccata variata, for ten wind instruments, piano and percussion (1931–2). fp Munich, 1932

Piano Sonata No. 1 (1932). fp Munich, 4 January 1933

String Quartet No. 1: *Carillon* (1933). fp Geneva, 1936

Piano Sonata No. 2: '27 April 1945' (1945). fp Munich, 13 June 1982

String Quartet No. 2 (1945–6). fp Milan, 1949

Scherzo for Percussion Ensemble (1956; unfinished, completion made by Wilfried Hiller). Unperformed

Choral

Profane Messe ('Secular Mass'), for mixed chorus unaccompanied, texts unknown (1928–9). fp?

Cantata for male chorus unaccompanied, texts by Becher and Marx (1930). fp?

Friede Anno 48, cantata for soprano, mixed chorus and piano, text by Andreas Gryphius (1936). fp Cologne, 22 October 1968

Vocal

Lamento, cantata for soprano and piano, text by Andreas Gryphius (1936–7, revised 1955). fp Constance, 26 May 1955

Ghetto, for alto, baritone and small orchestra, text by Jens Gerlach, Part 3 of *Jewish Chronicle* – collaborative work with Boris Blacher, Paul Dessau, Henze and Rudolf Wagner-Régeny (1960–61). fp Cologne, 14 January 1966

Gesangsszene ('Hymn-scene'), for baritone and orchestra, text by Jean Giraudoux (1962–3, unfinished). fp Frankfurt am Main, 12 November 1964

Hans Werner Henze

Works are listed according to the following categories: Opera, Ballet, Incidental Music for Theatre and Film, Vocal with Instruments, Vocal with Orchestra, Choral, Orchestral, Solo Instrument(s) with Orchestra, Chamber, Piano, Instrumental.

Opera

Das Wundertheater ('The Magic Theatre'), text from Miguel Cervantes (1948). fp Heidelberg, 7 May 1949. Revised version forming triple-bill with *Ein Landarzt* and *Das Ende einer Welt*, 1964. fp Frankfurt am Main, 30 November 1965

Boulevard Solitude, libretto by Grete Weil (1951) fp Hanover, 17 February 1952

Ein Landarzt ('A Country Doctor'), radio opera, libretto by the composer after Franz Kafka (1951). fp Hamburg, 19 November 1951; (stage) Cologne, 27 May 1953. Revised version forming triple-bill with *Das Wundertheater* and *Das Ende einer Welt*, 1964. fp Frankfurt am Main, 30 November 1965. Rewritten in 1965 as a Concert Monodrama for Baritone and Orchestra.

Das Ende einer Welt ('The End of a World'), radio opera, libretto by Wolfgang Hildesheimer (1953). fp Hamburg, 4 December 1953. Revised version forming triple-bill with *Das Wundertheater* and *Ein Landarzt*, 1964. fp Frankfurt am Main, 30 November 1965

König Hirsch ('King Stag'), libretto by Heinz von Cramer (1952–5). fp (cut) Berlin, 23 September 1956; (original version) Stuttgart, 5 May 1985. Reduced version, *Il Re Cervo or The Vagaries of Truth*, 1962. fp Kassel, 10 March 1963

Der Prinz von Homburg ('The Prince of Homburg'), libretto by Ingeborg Bachmann after Heinrich von Kleist (1958). fp Hamburg, 22 May 1960. Revised version, 1991. fp Munich, 14 July 1992

Elegy for Young Lovers, libretto by Wystan Hugh Auden and Chester Kallman (1959–61). fp Schwetzingen, 20 May 1961. Revised scoring, 1988. fp Venice, 28 October 1988

Der junge Lord ('The Young Lord'), comic opera, libretto by Ingeborg Bachmann after Wilhelm Hauff (1964). fp Berlin, 7 April 1965

The Bassarids, libretto by Wystan Hugh Auden and Chester Kallman (1964–5). fp Salzburg, 6 August 1966

The Judgment of Calliope, intermezzo for *The Bassarids*, libretto by Wystan Hugh Auden and Chester Kallman (1965). fp Salzburg, 6 August 1966

Moralities, three scenic cantatas, libretto by Wystan Hugh Auden (1967). fp Cincinnati, 18 May 1968

Der langwierige Weg in die Wohnung der Natascha Ungeheuer ('The Tedious Way to the Place of Natascha Frightful'), libretto by Gastón Salvatore (1971). fp Rome, 17 May 1971

La Cubana oder Ein Leben für die Kunst ('The Cuban Woman or A Life for the Arts'), Vaudeville, libretto by Hans Magnus Enzensberger after Miguel Barnet (1973). fp Munich, 28 May 1975. Revised version 1994–, in preparation

We come to the River, libretto by Edward Bond (1974–6). fp London, 12 July 1976

Don Chisciotte della Mancia ('Don Quixote from La Mancha'), comic opera by Giovanni Lorenzi and Giovanni Paisiello, new edition with Giuseppe di Leva (1976). fp Montepulciano, 1 August 1976

Pollicino, libretto by Giuseppe di Leva after Collodi, Grimm and Perrault (1979–80). fp Montepulciano, 2 August 1980

The English Cat, libretto by Edward Bond (1978–82). fp Schwetzingen, 2 June 1983

Il ritorno d'Ulisse in patria ('The Return of Ulysses to his Homeland') free reconstruction of Claudio Monteverdi's opera, libretto by Giacomo Badoaro (1981). fp Salzburg, 16 August 1985

Ödipus der Tyrann oder Der Vater vertreibt seinen Sohn und schickt die Tochter in die Küche ('Oedipus the Tyrant, or The father drives his son away and sends his daughter into the kitchen'), for tenor, guitar and string trio, with Hans-Jürgen von Bose, Simon Holt and David Lang (1983). fp Kindberg, 30 October 1983

Das verratene Meer ('The Betrayed Sea'), libretto by Hans-Ulrich Treichel after Yukio Mishima (1986–9). fp Berlin, 5 May 1990

Venus and Adonis, libretto by Hans-Ulrich Treichel after Shakespeare (1993–; in preparation)

Ballet

Ballet Variations (1949). fp (concert) Düsseldorf, 3 October 1949; (stage) Wuppertal, 21 December 1958

Jack Pudding (1949). fp Wiesbaden, 30 December 1950

Rosa Silber (1950). fp (concert) Berlin, 8 May 1951; (stage) Cologne, 15 October 1958

Die schlafende Prinzessin ('The Sleeping Princess') for small orchestra, after Tchaikovsky (1951). fp Essen, 5 June 1954

Labyrinth: Choreographic Fantasy (1951). fp (concert) Darmstadt, 29 May 1952

Der Idiot, mimed drama after Dostoevsky (1952). fp Berlin, 1 September 1952. Revised as *Paraphrase on Dostoevsky* for speaker and eleven instruments, 1990. fp London, 12 January 1991

Pas d'action (1952). fp Munich, 1952. Withdrawn, rewritten as *Tancredi*, 1964

Maratona di Danza ('Dance Marathon') (1956) fp Berlin, 24 September 1957

Undine (1956–7). fp London, 27 October 1958

Des Kaisers Nachtigall (L'Usignolo dell'Imperatore, 'The Emperor's Nightingale') (1959). fp Venice, 16 September 1959. Revised version with reduced scoring, 1970. fp Braunschweig, November 1970

Tancredi (1964, based on withdrawn *Pas d'action*, 1952). fp Vienna, 18 May 1966

Orpheus, text by Edward Bond (1978). fp Stuttgart, 17 March 1979. Revised version for Vienna, 1986. fp Vienna, 20 June 1986

Incidental Music for Theatre and Film

Incidental Music for Shakespeare's *Much Ado About Nothing* (1949). Unperformed. Re-used in Serenade for Solo Cello

Incidental Music for Beaumarchais' *La Folle Journée* (1951). Unperformed

Incidental Music for Musset's *Les Caprices de Marianne* (1962). fp Baden-Baden, January 1962

Muriel, film score (1963)

Incidental Music for Aristophanes' *The Peace* (Der Frieden) (1964). fp Munich, 20 September 1964

Der junge Törless ('The Young Törless'), film score (1966)

Die verlorene Ehre der Katharina Blum ('The Lost Honour of Katherina Blum'), film score (1975)

Incidental Music for Edward Bond's *The Woman* (1978)

Un amour de Swann, film score (1984)

Vocal with Instruments

Whispers from Heavenly Death, for voice and piano or eight instruments, text by Walt Whitman (1948). fp Hesse, 1950

Apollo et Hyazinthus, for harpsichord, alto and eight instruments, text by Georg Trakl (1949). fp Frankfurt am Main, 26 June 1949

Kammermusik 1958, for tenor, guitar (or harp) and eight instruments, text by Friedrich Hölderlin (1958). fp Hamburg, 26 November 1958. Revised version, 1963. fp Berlin, December 1963

Ariosi, for soprano, violin and piano four hands, text by Torquato Tasso (1963). fp Mannheim, 19 November 1965

Being Beauteous, cantata, for coloratura soprano, harp and four cellos, texts by Arthur Rimbaud (1963). fp Berlin, 12 April 1964

El Cimarrón, 'recital' for singer, flautist, guitarist and percussionist, libretto by Hans Magnus Enzensberger after Miguel Barnet (1969–70, revised 1979). fp Aldeburgh, 22 June 1970

El Rey de Harlem ('The King of Harlem')*: Imaginary Theatre I*, for singer and instrumental ensemble to a text by Federico Garcia Lorca (1979). fp Witten, 20 April 1980

Three Songs, for tenor and piano, on poems by Wystan Hugh Auden (1983). fp Aldeburgh, 15 June 1983

Drei Lieder über den Schnee ('Three Songs about Snow') for soprano, baritone and eight instruments, text by Hans-Ulrich Treichel (1989). fp Frankfurt am Main, 8 September 1989

Vocal with Orchestra

Der Vorwurf ('The Reproach'), concert aria, for baritone, trumpet, trombone and string orchestra, text by Franz Werfel (1948). fp Darmstadt, 29 July 1948

Fünf neapolitanische Lieder ('Five Neapolitan Songs') on anonymous seventeenth-century texts, for baritone and chamber orchestra (1956). fp Frankfurt am Main, 26 May 1956

Nachtstücke und Arien ('Nocturnes and Arias'), for soprano and large orchestra, on poems by Ingeborg Bachmann (1957). fp Donaueschingen, 20 October 1957

Ariosi for soprano, violin and orchestra, text by Torquato Tasso (1963). fp Edinburgh, 23 August 1964

Ein Landarzt ('A Country Doctor'), monodrama after Franz Kafka (1965, from Opera, 1951–64). fp Berlin, 13 October 1965

Versuch über Schweine ('Essay on Pigs'), for baritone and chamber orchestra, text by Gastón Salvatore (1968). fp London, 14 February 1969

Voices (Stimmen), song cycle, for two singers and instrumental groups, texts: Heberto Padilla, Ho Chi Minh, Bertolt Brecht, Victor Hernandez Cruz, Calvin C. Hernton, Erich Fried, Gino de Santis, Mario Tobino, Heinrich Heine, Giuseppe Ungaretti, Hans Magnus Enzensberger, Miguel Barnet, Walton Smith, Richard W. Thomas, Dudley Randall, F. C. Delius, Michaelis Katsaros (1973). fp London, 4 January 1974

Wesendonk-Lieder, arrangement of Richard Wagner's original score, for alto and chamber orchestra (1976). fp Cologne, 25 March 1977

Szenen und Arien aus »Il ritorno d'Ulisse in patria«: 'Scenes and Arias from Claudio Monteverdi's *The Return of Ulysses to his Homeland*' (1981). fp London, 4 September 1988

Two Concert Arias (freely adapted from *König Hirsch*), for tenor and small orchestra (1991). fp?

Songs and Dances from *La Cubana*, for mezzo-soprano and chamber ensemble (1993). fp London, 20 September 1994

Choral

Five Madrigals, for small mixed chorus and eleven instruments, on poems by François Villon (1947). fp Frankfurt am Main, 25 April 1950

Wiegenlied der Mutter Gottes ('Lullaby of the Blessed Virgin') for boys' chorus and nine instruments, texts by Lope de Vega (1948). fp Duisburg, 27 June 1954

Chor gefangener Trojer ('Chorus of the Captured Trojans'), for mixed choir and orchestra, text by J. W. Goethe (1948, revised 1964). fp Bielefeld, 6 February 1949

Aufstand ('Revolt'), for soloists, chorus and orchestra, text by Jens Gerlach, part of *Jewish Chronicle* – collaborative work with Boris Blacher, Paul Dessau, Hartmann and Rudolf Wagner-Régeny (1960–61). fp Cologne, 14 January 1966

Novae de infinito laudes ('New Praises of the Infinite'), cantata, for soloists, mixed chorus and small orchestra, text by Giordano Bruno (1962). fp Venice, 24 April 1963

Cantata della fiaba estrema, ('Song of the Final Fairy-Tale') for soprano, small chorus and ensemble, text by Elsa Morante (1963). fp Zürich, 26 February 1965

Choral Fantasy, for chamber choir, trombone, two cellos, double bass, percussion and timpani, text by Ingeborg Bachmann (1964). fp Selb, 23 January 1967

Musen Siziliens ('Sicilian Muses'), concerto for chorus, two pianos, wind and timpani, text by Virgil (1966). fp Berlin, 20 September 1966

Das Floß der »Medusa« ('The Raft of the "Medusa"') 'oratorio volgare e militare', text by Ernst Schnabel (1968). fp Vienna, 29 January 1971

Jephte, realization of Giacomo Carissimi's Oratorio, for soloists, chorus and orchestra (1976). fp London, 14 July 1976

Orpheus behind the Wire, for mixed chorus (unaccompanied), text by Edward Bond (1981–3). fp Southampton, 10 September 1985

Orchestral

Symphony No. 1, for chamber orchestra (1947). fp (movement II only) Darmstadt, 1947; (complete) Bad Pyrmont, 25 August 1948. Revised version, 1963. fp Berlin, 9 April 1964

Suite from the ballet *Jack Pudding,* for chamber orchestra (1949). fp Heidelberg, 23 June 1950

Symphony No. 2, for large orchestra (1949). fp Stuttgart, 1 December 1949

Symphony No. 3, for large orchestra (1949–50). fp Donaueschingen, 7 October 1951

Symphonic Variations (1950). fp Wiesbaden, 1950

Suite from the ballet *Pas d'action* (later *Tancredi*) (1952). fp Hamburg, 15 January 1953

Symphonic Interludes from the opera *Boulevard Solitude* (1953). fp Aachen, 7 June 1952

Quattro poemi (1955). fp Frankfurt am Main, 31 May 1955

Symphony No. 4, for large orchestra, adapted from *König Hirsch* (1955). fp Berlin, 9 October 1963

Three Symphonic Studies (1955, revised 1964). fp Hamburg, 14 February 1956

Suite from the ballet *Maratona di Danza,* for two jazz bands and orchestra (1956). fp Cologne, 8 February 1957

Hochzeitsmusik ('Wedding Music'), for symphonic wind band, from the ballet *Undine* (1957). fp 1959

Sonata for Strings (1957–8). fp Zürich, 21 March 1958

Suite No. 1 from the ballet *Undine* (1958). fp Stuttgart, April 1959

Suite No. 2 from the ballet *Undine* (1958). fp Mannheim, 3 March 1958

Three Dithyrambs, for chamber orchestra (1958). fp Cologne, 27 November 1958

Trois pas des Tritons from the ballet *Undine* (1958–9). fp Rome, 10 January 1959

Antifone ('Antiphony') (1960). fp Berlin, 20 January 1962

Symphony No. 5, for large orchestra (1962). fp New York, 16 May 1963

Los Caprichos, fantasia after Goya (1963). fp Duisburg, 6 April 1967

Zwischenspiele – Symphonic Interludes from *Der junge Lord* (1964). fp Berlin, 12 October 1965

In memoriam: Die weiße Rose ('The White Rose'), for small orchestra (1965). fp Bologna, 26 March 1965

Mänadenjagd ('The Hunt of the Maenads') from *The Bassarids* (1965). fp Bielefeld, 23 April 1971

Fantasia for String Orchestra or Sextet, from film music *Der junge Törless* (1966). fp Berlin, 1 April 1967

Telemanniana (1967). fp Berlin, 4 April 1967

Symphony No. 6, for two chamber orchestras (1969). fp Havana, Cuba, 26 November 1969

Heliogabalus Imperator, allegory for music (1971–2). fp Chicago, 16 November 1972. Revised version, 1986. fp Rome, 28 June 1988

Ragtimes and Habaneras, symphony for brass band (1975). fp London, 13 September 1975

Katharina Blum, concert suite for orchestra (1975). fp Brighton, Sussex, 6 May 1976

Aria de la folía española (1977). fp (version for chamber orchestra) St Paul, Minnesota, 17 September 1977; (version for orchestra) Bournemouth, 23 April 1979

Orpheus, concert version for speaker and orchestra (1978). fp Cologne, 4 March 1983

Arien des Orpheus ('Songs of Orpheus'), for guitar, harp and strings (1979). fp Gelsenkirchen, 16 November 1980. Version for large string orchestra, 1981. fp Chicago, 25 November 1981

Apollo trionfante ('Apollo Triumphant') from *Orpheus*, for wind, keyboard instruments, percussion and double basses (1979). fp Gelsenkirchen, 1 September 1980

Dramatic Scenes from *Orpheus*, for large orchestra (1979). fp (Set 1) Frankfurt am Main, 12 September 1982; (Set 2) Zürich, 6 January 1981

Barcarola (1979). fp Zürich, 22 April 1980

Spielmusiken ('Music to Play') from *Pollicino*, for old and modern instruments (1979–80). fp Montepulciano, 2 August 1980

Cinque piccoli concerti e ritornelli ('Five Little Concertos and Ritornellos') (1983). fp London, 24 January 1988

Symphony No. 7, for large orchestra (1983–4). fp Berlin, 1 December 1984

Deutschlandsberger Mohrentanz No. 1, for four recorders, guitar, percussion, string quartet and string orchestra (1984). fp Deutschlandsberg, Austria, 14 October 1984

Kleine Elegien ('Little Elegies'), for old instruments (1984–5). fp Cologne, 13 December 1986

Deutschlandsberger Mohrentanz No. 2, for four recorders, guitar, percussion, string quartet and string orchestra (1985). fp Deutschlandsberg, Austria, 19 October 1985

Fandango sopra un basso del Padre Soler (1985). fp Paris, 5 February 1986

Allegro brillante (1987–9). fp Dallas, Texas, 14 September 1989

Theater und Salonmusik, from mime-drama *Der Idiot* (1952, arranged 1989). fp Bristol, 5 June 1989

La selva incantata ('The Enchanted Wood'), from *König Hirsch* (1991). fp ?

Symphony No. 8 (1991–3). fp Boston, Mass., 1 October 1993

Orchestration of Hartmann's Piano Sonata No. 2 '27 April 1945' (in preparation)

Symphony No. 9 (in preparation for 1996)

Solo Instrument(s) with Orchestra

Chamber Concerto, for piano, flute and strings (1946). fp Darmstadt, 27 September 1946

Concertino for Piano and Wind Orchestra with Percussion (1947). fp Baden-Baden, 5 October 1947

Violin Concerto No. 1 (1947). fp Baden-Baden, 12 December 1948

Piano Concerto No. 1 (1950). fp Düsseldorf, 14 September 1952

Ode an den Westwind ('Ode to the West Wind'), music for cello and orchestra (1953). fp Bielefeld, 30 April 1954

Concerto per il Marigny, for piano and seven instruments (1956). fp Paris, 9 March 1956

Jeux des Tritons, divertissement from the ballet *Undine* for piano and orchestra (1956–7, revised 1967). fp Zürich, 28 March 1960

Double Concerto, for oboe, harp and strings (1966). fp Zürich, 2 December 1966

Concerto for Double Bass and Orchestra (1966). fp Chicago, 2 November 1967

Piano Concerto No. 2 (1967). fp Bielefeld, 29 September 1968

Compases para preguntas ensimismadas ('Questions Asked of One's Soul'), music for viola and twenty-two instruments (1969–70). fp ?

Violin Concerto No. 2, for solo violin, tape, bass-baritone and thirty-three instruments, text by Hans Magnus Enzensberger (1971). fp Basel, 2 November 1972

Tristan, preludes for piano, tape and orchestra (1973). fp London, 20 October 1974

Il Vitalino raddoppiato, chaconne for violin and chamber orchestra (1977). fp Salzburg, 2 August 1978

Le Miracle de la rose: Imaginary Theatre II, for clarinet and thirteen players (1981). fp London, 26 May 1982

I Sentimenti di Carl Philipp Emanuel Bach, transcription for flute, harp and strings (1982). fp Rome, 14 April 1982

Konzertstück ('Concert Piece'), for cello and small orchestra (1977–85). fp Frankfurt am Main, 29 August 1986

Sieben Liebeslieder ('Seven Love-songs'), for cello and orchestra (1984–5). fp Cologne, 12 December 1986

An eine Äolsharfe ('To an Aeolian Harp') for guitar and fifteen instruments (1985–6). fp Lucerne, 27 August 1986

Introduction, Theme and Variations, for cello, harp and strings, extracted from *Konzertstück* (1992) and last movement of *Liebeslieder*. fp ?

Requiem, Nine Sacred Concertos, for piano, trumpet and chamber orchestra (1990–93) fp Berlin, 27 February 1993

Chamber

String Quartet (1945–6). fp Braunschweig, 1947

String Quartet No. 1 (1947). fp Heidelberg, 1947

Chamber Sonata, for piano, violin and cello (1948, revised 1963). fp Cologne, 16 March 1950

String Quartet No. 2 (1952). fp Baden-Baden, 16 December 1952

Wind Quintet (1952). fp Bremen, 15 February 1953

Quattro Fantasie ('Four Fantasias') from *Kammermusik 1958*, for clarinet, bassoon, horn, two violins, viola, cello and double bass (1963). fp?

Fragmente aus einer Show ('Fragments from a Show') from *Der langwierige Weg in die Wohnung der Natascha Ungeheuer*, for brass quintet (1971). fp USA, October 1971

Carillon, Récitatif, Masque, trio for mandolin, guitar and harp (1974). fp London, 2 February 1977

String Quartet No. 3 (1975–6). fp Berlin, 12 September 1976

Amicizia, ('Friendship'), quintet for clarinet in A, trombone, cello, percussion and piano (1976). fp Montepulciano, 6 August 1976

String Quartet No. 4 (1976). fp Schwetzingen, 25 May 1977

String Quartet No. 5 (1976). fp Schwetzingen, 25 May 1977

L'Autunno ('Autumn'), for wind quintet (1977). fp London, 28 February 1979

Canzona, for oboe, three violas, cello, piano and harp (1982). fp Stuttgart, 6 June 1982

Sonata per otto ottoni, for high trumpet in G, two trumpets in B flat, flügelhorn, bass trumpet, two tenor trombones and bass trombone (1983). fp Berlin, 17 September 1983

Sonata for Six Players (1984). fp London, 26 September 1984

Selbst- und Zwiegespräche, trio for viola, guitar and organ or other keyboard instrument (1984–5). fp Brühl, 29 September 1985

Piano Quintet (1990–1). fp Berkeley, California, 25 March 1993

Three Mozart Organ Sonatas, arranged for fourteen players (1991). fp Frankfurt am Main, 19 September 1991

Adagio adagio, serenade for piano, violin and cello (1993). fp Darmstadt, 18 March 1993

Piano

Variations, Op. 13 (1949). fp Frankfurt am Main, 17 June 1949

Sonata (1959). fp Berlin, 26 September 1959

Lucy Escott Variations, for piano or harpsichord (1963). fp (both versions) Berlin, 21 March 1965

Divertimenti for Two Pianos (1964). fp New York, 30 November 1964

Sechs Stücke für junge Pianisten ('Six Pieces for Young Pianists') from *Pollicino* (1980). fp Stuttgart, 13 October 1982

Cherubino, three miniatures for piano (1980–81). fp Berlin, 23 August 1981

Une petite phrase for the film *Un amour de Swann* (1984). fp?

La mano sinistra ('The Left Hand') for piano, left hand (1988). fp?

Toccata mistica (1994). fp Cologne, 13 November 1994

Instrumental

Sonata for Violin and Piano (1946). fp?

Sonatina for Flute and Piano (1947). fp Darmstadt, 1947

Serenade for Solo Cello (1949; adapted from incidental music to *Much Ado About Nothing*). fp 1950

Three Tentos from *Kammermusik 1958*, for solo guitar (1958). fp Hamburg, 26 November 1958

Six Absences, for harpsichord (1961). fp Mainz, 7 November 1963

Sonatina for Solo Trumpet (1974). fp?

Royal Winter Music, First Sonata on Shakespearean Characters, for solo guitar (1975–6). fp Berlin, 20 September 1976

Character Studies from *Don Chisciotte della Mancia* for two guitars (1976). fp?

Sonata for Solo Violin (1976–7). fp Montepulciano, 10 August 1977

S. Biagio 9 Agosto ore 1207, record for solo double bass (1977). fp?

Five Scenes from the Snow Country, for solo marimba (1978). fp Stuttgart, 12 October 1982

Toccata senza Fuga ('Toccata without Fugue'), from *Orpheus*, for organ (1979). fp Stuttgart, 21 May 1979

Royal Winter Music, Second Sonata on Shakespearean Characters, for solo guitar (1979). fp Brussels, 25 November 1980

Sonatina from the opera *Pollicino*, for violin and piano (1979). fp London, 2 December 1980

Etude philharmonique, for solo violin (1979). fp?

Sonata for Viola and Piano (1979). fp Witten, 20 April 1980

Capriccio for Solo Cello (or Double Bass) (1976–81). fp Linz, 24 September 1983

Euridice, fragments for harpsichord (1981). fp?

Serenade for Solo Violin (1986). fp Bad Godesberg, 1 June 1986

Für Manfred, for solo violin (1989). fp Cologne, 12 September 1989

Fünf Nachtstücke ('Five Nocturnes'), for violin and piano (1990). fp London, 16 May 1990

Paul Hindemith

This list does not include the numerous juvenilia and student works that preceded Hindemith's official opus 1, the *Andante and Scherzo* of 1914. Also omitted are various sketches, pastiches (most of which have disappeared) and minor pieces created for use in Hindemith's composition classes and not intended for public consumption. Most of the early pre-opus 1 compositions did not survive World War II, nor did certain of the works with opus numbers. My thanks are due once again to Dr Giselher Schubert of the Paul Hindemith Institute for his help in the preparation of this list.

Works are listed according to the following categories: Opera, Ballet, Film Music, Choral (unaccompanied), Choral with Orchestra, Vocal with Piano, Vocal with Instruments/Orchestra, Orchestral, Solo Instrument(s) with Orchestra, Chamber, Piano, Instrumental.

Opera

Mörder, Hoffnung der Frauen ('Murder, Hope of Women'), Op. 12, text by Oskar Kokoschka (1919). fp Stuttgart, 4 June 1921

Das Nusch-Nuschi, Op. 20, text by Franz Blei (1920). fp Stuttgart, 4 June 1921

Sancta Susanna, Op. 21, text by August Stramm (1921). fp Frankfurt am Main, 26 March 1922

Tuttifäntchen, children's Christmas opera, text by Hedwig Michel and Franziska Becker (1922). fp Darmstadt, 13 December 1922

Cardillac, Op. 39, libretto by Ferdinand Lion, after E. T. A. Hoffmann (1926). fp Dresden, 9 November 1926. Revised version, 1952, libretto by the composer. fp Zürich, 20 June 1952

Hin und zurück ('There and Back'), Op. 45a, libretto by Marcellus Schiffer (1927). fp Baden-Baden, 15 July 1927

Neues vom Tage ('Today's News'), libretto by Marcellus Schiffer (1928–9). fp Berlin, 8 June 1929. Revised version, 1953. fp Naples, 7 April 1954

Wir bauen eine Stadt ('Let's Build a Town'), libretto by Robert Seitz (1930). fp Berlin, 21 June 1930

Mathis der Maler ('Mathis the Painter'), libretto by the composer (1933–5). fp Zürich, 28 May 1938

Die Harmonie der Welt ('The Harmony of the World'), libretto by the composer (1956–7). fp Munich, 11 August 1957

Das lange Weihnachtsmahl ('The Long Christmas Dinner') libretto by Thornton Wilder (1960). fp Mannheim, Germany, 17 December 1961

Ballet

Der Dämon ('The Demon'), Op. 28 (1922). fp Darmstadt, 1 December 1923

Das Triadische Ballett ('The Triadic Ballet'), for mechanical piano, Op. 40 No. 2 (1926). fp Donaueschingen, 1926

Nobilissima Visione (1938). fp London, 21 July 1938

Theme with Four Variations: *The Four Temperaments*, for piano and string orchestra (1940). fp (concert) Boston, Mass., 3 September 1940; (staged) New York, 20 November 1946

Hérodiade (1944). fp Washington, DC, 30 October 1944

Film Music

Im kämpf dem Berge ('A Struggle with the Mountain'; also *In Sturm und Eis*, 'In Storm and Ice'), for large chamber ensemble (1921). fp 1922 (on release of film)

Felix the Cat at the Circus, for mechanical organ (1927; lost). fp Baden-Baden, 16 July 1927

Vormittagspuk ('Haunting in the Morning'), for pianola (1928). fp Baden-Baden, 14 July 1928

Music for a Cartoon, for piano (1931; lost). fp?

Music for an Abstract Cartoon, for string trio (1931; lost). fp?

Clermont and Fouet, music for an advertisement, for string trio (1931; lost). fp?

Music for a film by Fischinger, for solo violin (1932; lost). fp?

Choral (unaccompanied)

Seven Songs on Old Texts, Op. 33, for mixed chorus, texts: Martin Luther, Burggraf zu Regensburg, Spervogel, Heinrich von Morungen, Reinmar, Anon. (1923). fp (Nos. 1–2, 5–7) Donaueschingen, 27 July 1925

Lieder für Singkreise, Op. 43 No. 2, for mixed chorus , texts: Platen, Rainer Maria Rilke, Matthias Claudius (1927). fp?

Spruch eines Fahrenden ('A Traveller's Saying'), for female chorus, text: Anon. (1928). fp?

Three Canons, for female chorus, texts: Hrabanus Maurus, Anon., Martin Luther (1928). fp?

Thirty Canons, for various vocal combinations (2–11 vv; male chorus), texts: various (1928–63). fpp?

Über das Frühjahr ('Concerning Spring'), for male chorus, text by Bertolt Brecht (1929). fp?

Eine lichte Mitternacht ('A light Midnight'), for male chorus, text by Walt Whitman (1929). fp?

Fürst Kraft ('Prince Strength'), for male chorus, text by Gottfried Benn (1930). fp Vienna, May 1931

Du mußt dir alles geben ('You Must Give Yourself Everything'), for male chorus, text by Gottfried Benn (1930). fp Vienna, May 1931

Vision des Mannes ('Vision of the Man'), for male chorus, text by Gottfried Benn (1930). fp?

Choral Songs, for boys' chorus, text by Karl Schnog (1930). fp?

Der Tod ('Death'), for male chorus, text by Friedrich Hölderlin (1931). fp?

Five Songs on Old Texts, for mixed chorus, texts: Heinrich von Veldeke, Burggraf zu Regensburg, Martin Luther, Anon., Spervogel (1937). (Nos. 2–5 revised versions of Seven Songs on old Texts, Nos. 2, 1, 6 and 3). fp?

Three Choruses, for male chorus, texts: 1 and 3 anonymous, 2 by Friedrich Nietzsche (1939). fp Ostend, Belgium, August 1939

Erster Schnee ('First Snow'), for male chorus, text by Gottfried Keller (1939). fp?

Variations on an Old Dancing Song, for male chorus, text: anonymous (1939). fp?

The Demon of the Gibbet, for male chorus, text by Fritz-James O'Brien (1939). fp?

Six Chansons on original French poems by Rainer Maria Rilke, for mixed chorus (1939). fp Amsterdam, 1939

Musica divinas laudes, canon for female chorus, text: anonymous (1949). fp? Later combined with the Three Canons, 1928, as Four Canons, 1928–49

Twelve Madrigals, for mixed chorus, texts by Josef Weinheber (1958). fp Vienna, 18 October 1958

Mass (1963). fp Vienna, 12 November 1963

Choral with Orchestra
(except where stated otherwise)

Lügenlied ('Song of Lies'), for mixed chorus, strings and woodwinds (1928). fp?

Frau Musica ('Lady Music'), Op. 45 No. 1, cantata, text by Martin Luther (1928). fp Nuremberg, 27 March 1929. Revised as *In Praise of Music*, 1943. fp New York, November 1945

Wer sich die Musik erkiest ('He who Chooses Music for Himself'), Op. 45 No. 2, canon for mixed chorus and string quartet (from Eight Canons) (1928). fp?

Badener Lehrstück vom Einverständnis, ('Baden's Lesson on Consensus') scenic cantata, text by Bertolt Brecht (1929). fp Baden-Baden, 28 July 1929

Das Lindberghflug ('Lindbergh's Flight') six movements for cantata composed with Kurt Weill, text by Bertolt Brecht (1929). fp Baden-Baden, 27 July 1929

Das Unaufhörliche ('The Perpetual'), oratorio, text by Gottfried Benn (1931). fp Berlin, 21 November 1931

Mahnung an die Jugend, sich der Musik zu befleißigen ('Warning to Youth to Take up Music'), cantata for speaker, youth choir and string orchestra, with woodwinds and percussion ad lib., text by Martin Agricola (from *Plöner Musiktag,* 1932). fp Plön, 20 June 1932

Old Irish Song, *The Harp that once thro' Tara's Halls,* text: anonymous, for mixed chorus and piano or harp and strings (1940). fp?

Lied von der Musik ('A Song of Music'), for women's chorus and piano or strings, text by George Tyler (1941). fp?

When Lilacs Last in the Door-Yard Bloom'd: A Requiem 'For Those We Loved', text drawn by the composer from Walt Whitman (1946). fp New York, 5 May 1946

Apparebit repentina dies, for chorus and brass, texts: anonymous (1947). fp Cambridge, Mass., May 1947

Ite, angeli veloces, cantata, text by Paul Claudel (1953–5). fp Wuppertal, Germany, 4 June 1955

Mainzer Umzug ('The Procession of Mainz'), text by Carl Zuckmayer and Hindemith (1962). fp Mainz, Germany, 23 June 1962

Vocal with Piano

(without chorus; solo voice except where stated otherwise)

Lieder in Aargauer Mundart ('Songs in the Aargauer Dialect'), texts: Sofie Hämmerli-Marti, Adolf Frey, Josef Reinhart, Op. 5 (1916). fp?

Two Songs, for alto and piano, texts by Else Lasker-Schüller, (*c.* 1918). fp?

Three Hymns of Walt Whitman, Op. 14 (1919). fp Frankfurt am Main, 26 February 1920

Eight Songs, Op. 18, texts: Curt Bock, Christian Morgenstern, Else Lasker-Schüller, Heinar Schilling, Georg Trakl (1920). fp Berlin, 25 January 1922

Das Kind ('The Child'), text by Friedrich von Hagedorn (1922). fp?

Das Marienleben ('The Life of Mary'), song cycle on poems by Rainer Maria Rilke, Op. 27 (1922–3). fp Frankfurt am Main, 22 June 1923. Revised version, 1936–42. fp Hanover, 3 November 1948

Eight Canons, Op. 45 No. 2, for two voices and string quartet, texts: Anon., Martin Luther, Reinhard Goering, Christian Morgenstern, Franz Werfel, Jakob Kneip, Hermann Claudius, (1928). fp?

Four Songs on poems by Matthias Claudius (1933). fp?

Four Songs on poems by Rückert (1933). fp?

Four Songs on poems by Novalis (1933). fp?

Three Songs on poems by Wilhelm Busch (1933; lost). fp?

Six Songs on poems by Friedrich Hölderlin (1933–5). fp Frankfurt am Main, 4 November 1964

Four Songs on poems by Angelus Silesius (1935). fp?

Three Songs, texts: Clemens Brentano, Gottfried Keller (1936). fp?

Der Einsiedler ('The Settler'), text by Agostino da Cruz, translated by Karl Vossler (1939). fp?

Four Songs on poems by Friedrich Nietzsche (1936). fp?

Nine Songs for an American school songbook, on various texts (1938– 9). fp?

Thirteen Motets, texts: various (1941–60). fp Nos. 2, 8 and 11: Vienna, 2 April 1951; Nos. 3, 5, 9 and 13: Berlin, 2 October 1960; Nos. 1, 4, 6, 10 and 12: Venice, 13 April 1961

Two Ballads, texts: John Keats, Arthur Rimbaud (1942–4). fp?

Songs, for soprano and piano, on French and German texts by Burggraf zu Regensburg, Rainer Maria Rilke, Eichendorff, C.F. Meyer, Clemens Brentano, Platen, Lafontaine, Phaedrus, Gottfried Keller, Anon., Dautendey, Mallarmé, Baudelaire, (1942–4). fpp?

Nine English Songs, texts by Charles Wolfe, Thomas Moore, Percy Bysshe Shelley, William Oldys, Samuel Lover, Francis Thompson, William Blake, Walt Whitman, Robert Herrick (1942–4). fp?

The Expiring Frog: recitative and aria romantica, texts: Encyclopedia Britanica, Charles Dickens (1944). fp New Haven, Connecticut, 16 April 1944
Two Songs, text by Oscar Cox (1955). fp?

Vocal with Instruments/Orchestra

Three Orchestral Songs, Op. 9, texts: E. W. Lotz, Else Lasker-Schüller, (1917). fp Frankfurt am Main, 6 September 1974

Melancholie, Op. 13 for alto and string quartet, text by Christian Morgenstern, (1918). fp?

Wie es wär', wenn's anders wär ('How It Would Be If Things Were Otherwise'), for soprano and eight instruments, text by von Miris, (*c.* 1918). fp?

The Atonal Cabaret, text by Franz Wedekind, for solo voices and ensemble (1921; lost). fp?

Des Todes Tod ('The Death of Death'), Op. 23a, text by Eduard Reinacher, (1922). fp (private) Berlin, 24 February 1922; (public) Berlin, 7 March 1922

Die junge Magd ('The Young Maid'), Op. 23 No. 2, text by Georg Trakl (1922). fp Donaueschingen, 31 June 1922

Die Serenaden ('The Serenades'), small cantata, Op. 35 (1924). fp Winterthür, Switzerland, 15 April 1925

Martinslied ('Martin's Song'), Op. 45 No. 5, for solo voice (or unison chorus) and three instruments (strings or wind orchestra, one high, one middle, one bass), text by Johannes Olorinus (1929). fp?

Six Orchestral Songs from *Das Marienleben,* Op. 27 (1939–59). fp Nos. 1–4: Scheveningen, Switzerland, 13 August 1939; Nos. 5–6: Copenhagen, 21 September 1959

Orchestral

Lustige Sinfonietta in D minor, Op. 4 (1916). fp Berlin, 14 September 1980

Ragtime (wohltemperiert) ('Well-tempered Ragtime') (1921). fp Berlin, 21 March 1987

Nusch-Nuschi-Tänze, Dance Suite from *Nusch-Nuschi*, Op. 20 (1921). fp?

Kammermusik ('Chamber Music') No. 1 with '1921' Finale, Op. 24 No. 1 (1921). fp Donaueschingen, 31 July 1922

Chamber Symphony (1922; unfinished, first movement only). Unperformed

Der Dämon, Op. 28, concert suite from the ballet (1922, arranged 1923). fp?

Concerto, Op. 38 (1925). fp Duisburg, Germany, 25 July 1925

Konzertmusik, Op. 41, for wind orchestra (1926). fp Donaueschingen, 24 July 1926

Spielmusik ('Music to play'), Op. 43 No. 1, for string orchestra, flutes and oboes, Op. 43 No. 1 (1927). fp?

Five Pieces for String Orchestra, Op. 44 No. 4 (1927). fp?

Ein Jäger aus Kurpfalz ('A Hunter from Kurpfalz'), Op. 45 No. 3, *Spielmusik* for strings and wind orchestra, (1928). fp Nuremberg, 27 March 1929

Neues vom Tage, concert overture from the opera (1930). fp Nuremberg, 22 January 1930

Konzertmusik, Op. 50, for string orchestra and brass instruments, (1930). fp Boston, Mass., 4 April 1931

Philharmonic Concerto (1932). fp Berlin, 14 April 1932

Orchestral Concert from *Plöner Musiktag* ('Plön's Day of Music') (1932). fp Plön, 20 June 1932

Tafelmusik ('Table Music'), for flute, trumpet and string orchestra (from *Plöner Musiktag*, 1932). fp Plön, 20 June 1932

Mathis der Maler Symphony (1934). Berlin, 12 March 1934

Symphonic Dances (1937). fp London, 5 December 1937

Nobilissima Visione, suite (1938). fp Venice, 13 September 1938

Symphony in E flat (1940). fp Minneapolis, 21 November 1941

Amor and Psyche (Farnesina) (1943). fp Philadelphia, 29 October 1943

Symphonic Metamorphoses on Themes by Carl Maria von Weber (1943). fp New York, 20 January 1944

When Lilacs Last in the Door-Yard Bloom'd, prelude (1946). fp New York, 5 May 1946

Symphonia serena (1946). fp Dallas, Texas, 1 February 1947

Sinfonietta in E (1949–50). fp Louisville, Kentucky, 1 March 1950

Symphony in B flat for Wind Orchestra (1951). fp Washington, DC, 5 April 1951

Die Harmonie der Welt Symphony (1951). fp Basel, Switzerland, 25 January 1952

Suite französischer Tänze ('Suite of French Dances' after Pierre d'Attaignant) (1958). fp 23 September 1958

Pittsburgh Symphony (1958). fp Pittsburgh, 31 January 1959

March (1960). fp Basel, Switzerland, 30 June 1960

Solo Instrument(s) with Orchestra

Cello Concerto in E flat, Op. 3 (1915). fp Frankfurt am Main, 28 June 1916

Klaviermusik mit orchester, for piano (left hand) and orchestra (1923). fp?

Tuttifäntchen, suite from the opera for violin and small orchestra (1923). fp?

Kammermusik ('Chamber Music') No. 2, Op. 36 No. 1 Piano Concerto (1924). fp Frankfurt am Main, 31 October 1924

Kammermusik No. 3, Op. 36 No. 2, Cello Concerto (1925). fp Bochum, Germany, 30 April 1925

Kammermusik No. 4, Op. 36 No. 3, Violin Concerto (1925). fp Dessau, 25 September 1925

Kammermusik No. 5, Op. 36 No. 4, Viola Concerto (1927, first movement revised 1951). fp Berlin, 3 November 1927

Kammermusik No. 6, Op. 46 No. 1, Viola d'amore Concerto (1927). fp Cologne, 29 March 1928

Kammermusik No. 7, Op. 46 No. 2, Organ Concerto (1927). fp Frankfurt am Main, 8 January 1928

Konzertmusik ('Concert Music'), Op. 48, for viola and orchestra (1930). fp Hamburg, 28 March 1930

Konzertmusik, Op. 49, for piano, brass and two harps (1930). fp Chicago, 12 October 1930

Konzertstück ('Concert Piece'), for trautonium and strings (1931). fp Munich, 7 June 1931

Der Schwanendreher ('The Swan-turner'), concerto on old folk-songs for viola and small orchestra (1935). fp Amsterdam, 14 November 1935

Trauermusik, for viola (or violin or cello) and strings (1936). fp London, 22 January 1936 Violin Concerto (1939). fp Amsterdam, 14 March 1940

Cello Concerto (1940). fp Boston, Mass., 7 February 1941

Piano Concerto (1945). fp Cleveland, Ohio, 27 February 1947

Clarinet Concerto (1947). fp Philadelphia, 11 December 1950

Concerto for Woodwind, Harp and Orchestra (1949). fp New York, 15 May 1949

Horn Concerto (1949). fp Baden-Baden, 8 June 1950

Concerto for Trumpet and Bassoon with String Orchestra (1949). fp New Haven, Conn., 4 November 1949

Organ Concerto (1962). fp New York, 25 April 1963

Chamber

Andante and Scherzo, Op. 1, for clarinet, horn and piano, (1914). fp Frankfurt am Main, 12 June 1914

String Quartet in C major, Op. 2 (1915). fp Frankfurt am Main, 26 April 1915

Piano Quintet in E minor, Op. 7 (1917). fp Frankfurt am Main, 6 March 1918

String Quartet No. 1 in F minor, Op. 10 (1918). fp Frankfurt am Main, 2 June 1919

String Quartet No. 2 in C major, Op. 16 (1920). fp Donaueschingen, 1 August 1921

String Quartet No. 3, Op. 22 (1921). fp Donaueschingen, 4 November 1922

Kleine Kammermusik ('Little Chamber Music'), Op. 24 No. 2, for wind quintet, (1922). fp Cologne, 12 July 1922

Minimax – Repertorium für Militärmusik, for string quartet (1923). fp Donaueschingen, 26 July 1923

Overture to the Flying Dutchman as it is Played at Sight by a Bad Spa Band at 7 in the Morning by the Spring, for string quartet (1923). fp?

Quintet for Clarinet and String Quartet, Op. 30 (1923, revised 1954). fp Salzburg, 7 August 1923

String Quartet No. 4, Op. 32 (1923). fp Vienna, 5 November 1923

String Trio No. 1, Op. 34 (1924). fp Salzburg, 6 August 1924

Three Pieces for Five Instruments, clarinet, trumpet, violin, double bass, piano (1925; from *Three Anecdotes for Radio*). fp Frankfurt am Main, 18 February 1926

Trio for Flute, Clarinet and Double Bass (1927). fp?

Eight Pieces, Op. 44 No. 3, for two violins, viola, cello and double bass, (1927). fp?

Trio, Op. 47, for viola, heckelphone (or tenor saxophone) and piano, (1928). fp Wiesbaden, 15 March 1928

Morgenmusik ('Morning Music'), for brass instruments (from *Plöner Musiktag*, 1932). fp Plön, 20 June 1932

Trio for Three Recorders (from *Plöner Musiktag*, 1932). fp Plön, 20 June 1932

String Trio No. 2 (1933). fp Antwerp, 17 March 1933

Seven *Unterhaltungsstücke* ('Conversation Pieces'), for three clarinets (1934; lost). fp?

Quartet for Clarinet, Violin, Cello and Piano (1938). fp New York, 23 April 1939

Recorder Trio (*c.* 1942). fp?

String Quartet No. 5 in E flat (1943). fp Washington, DC, 7 November 1943

String Quartet No. 6 in E flat (1945). fp Washington, DC, 21 March 1946

Septet for Wind Instruments, flute, oboe, clarinet, bass clarinet, bassoon, horn and trumpet (1948). fp Milan, 30 December 1948

Sonata for Four Horns (1952). fp Vienna, June 1953

Octet for Clarinet, Bassoon, Horn, Violin, two Violas, Cello and Double Bass (1957–8). fp Berlin, 23 September 1958

Piano
(solo, except where stated otherwise)

Eight Waltzes, for piano duet, Op. 6 (1916). fp Frankfurt am Main, 18 December 1916

Two Marches, for piano duet (*c.* 1917). fp?

In einer Nacht.../Träume und Erlebnisse ('In one night/Dreams and Experiences'), Op. 15, suite (1919). fp Stuttgart, 28 February 1920

Five Further Pieces (1919). fp?

Sonata, Op. 17 (1920; MS. lost, reconstructed by Bernhard Billetter). fp (original) unperformed; (reconstruction) Switzerland, 1989

Tanzstücke ('Dance Pieces'), Op. 19 (1921). fp Dresden, 22 September 1924

Berceuse (1921). fp?

Klavierstück ('Piano Piece') *für Fraulein Paula Alsberg* (1921; lost). fp?

Lied ('Song') (1921). fp?

Suite '1922', Op. 26 (1922). fp Hanover, 3 December 1922

Klaviermusik ('Piano Music'), Op. 37 (1925–7). fp (Part 1) Dresden, November 1925; (Part 2) Dresden, April 1927. Rondo from Part 1, arranged for mechanical piano (1926). fp Donaueschingen, 25 July 1926

Kleine Klaviermusik ('Little Piano Music'), Op. 45 No. 4 (1929). fp?

Klavierstück ('Piano Piece') *für Frau Josefine Grosz* (1929). fp?

Wir bauen eine Stadt ('Let's Build a Town'), pieces for children (1931). fp?

Two Little Pieces (also Two Movements) (1934). fp?

Sonata No. 1 in A: *Der Main* ('The River Main') (1936). fp?

Sonata No. 2 in G (1936). fp?

Sonata No. 3 in B flat (1936). fp Washington, DC, 10 April 1937

Variations (original 2nd movement of Sonata No. 1, 1936). fp?

Sonata for Piano, four hands (1938). fp Zürich, 6 November 1938

Sonata for Two Pianos (1942). fp New York, 20 November 1942

Ludus tonalis (1942). fp Chicago, 15 February 1943

Instrumental

Sonata in G minor for Solo Violin, Op. 11 No. 6 (1917). fp Limburg, 1917

Three Movements for Cello and Piano, Op. 8 (1917). fp Frankfurt am Main, 6 March 1917

Two Movements for Organ (*c.* 1917–8). fp?

Sonata (No. 1) in E flat for Violin and Piano, Op. 11 No. 1 (1918). fp Frankfurt am Main, 2 June 1919

Sonata (No. 2) in D for Violin and Piano, Op. 11 No. 2 (1918). fp Frankfurt am Main, 10 April 1920

Sonata (No. 1) for Cello and Piano, Op. 11 No. 3 (1919). fp Frankfurt am Main, 27 October 1919. Revised version (1921). fp Munich, 5 January 1922

Sonata No. 1 in F for Viola and Piano, Op. 11 No. 4 (1919). fp Frankfurt am Main, 2 June 1919

Sonata for Solo Viola No. 1, Op. 11 No. 5 (1919). fp Friedberg, 14 November 1920

Sonata for Solo Viola No. 2, Op. 25 No. 1 (1922). fp Cologne 18 March 1922

Little Sonata for Viola d'amore and Piano, Op. 25 No.2 (1922). fp Heidelberg, June 1922

Sonata for Solo Cello, Op. 25 No. 3 (1922). fp Freiburg, 1923

Sonata No. 2 for Viola and Piano, Op. 25 No. 4 (1922). fp Elberfeld-Barmen, 10 January 1923

Sonata for Solo Viola No. 3, Op. 31 No. 4 (1923). fp Donaueschingen, 18 May 1924

Canonic Sonatina for Two Flutes, Op. 31 No. 3 (1923). fp?

Sonata for Solo Violin, Op. 31 No. 1 (1924). fp Donaueschingen, 21 March 1924

Sonata for Solo Violin, Op. 31 No. 2 (1924). fp Cologne, January 1927

Rondo for Two or Three Guitars (1925). fp Berlin, 21 June 1930

Toccata, Op. 40 No. 1, for Mechanical Piano (1926). fp Donaueschingen, 16 July 1927

Studies for Solo Violin (1926). fp?

Das triadische Ballett, Act 1, suite for mechanical organ (1926–7). fp Baden-Baden, 16 July 1927

Eight Pieces for Solo Flute (1927). fp?

Nine Movements for Clarinet and Double Bass (1927). fp?

Nine Pieces for Two Violins, Op. 44 No. 1 (1927). fp?

Eight Canons for Two Violins, Op. 44 No. 2 (1927). fp?

Seven Movements for Three Trautoniums (1930). fp Berlin, 20 June 1930

Two *Gramophone-Pieces*, for xylophone and voice (1930). fp Berlin, 18 June 1930

Forty-four Pieces for One or Two Violins (1931). fp?

Two Canonic Duets for Two Violins (1931). fp?

Canonic Variations for Two Violas (1932). fp?

Konzertstück ('Concert Piece') for Two Alto Saxophones (1933). fp?

Duet (Scherzo) for Viola and Cello (1934). fp London, 23 January 1934

Sonata (No. 3) in E for Violin and Piano (1935). fp Geneva, 18 February 1936

Langsames Stück und Rondo ('Adagio and Rondo'), for trautonium (1935; lost, reconstructed by Oscar Sala). fp?

Duet for Bassoon and Double Bass (1935; lost). fp?

Sonata for Flute and Piano (1936). fp Washington, DC, 10 April 1937

Sonata No. 4 for Solo Viola (1937). fp Chicago, 21 April 1937

Organ Sonata No. 1 (1937). fp London, 18 January 1938

Organ Sonata No. 2 (1937). fp London, 18 January 1938

Meditation, from the ballet *Nobilissima Visione*, for violin (or viola or cello) and piano (1938). fp?

Three Easy Pieces for Cello and Piano (1938). fp?

Sonata for Bassoon and Piano (1938). fp Zürich, 6 November 1938

Sonata for Oboe and Piano (1938). fp London, 20 July 1938

Sonata No. 3 for Viola and Piano (1938–9). fp Harvard University, Cambridge, Mass., 19 April 1939

Sonata (No. 4) in C for Violin and Piano (1939). fp?

Sonata for Clarinet and Piano (1939). fp?

Sonata for Harp (1939). fp?

Sonata for Horn and Piano (1939). fp?

Sonata for Trumpet (in B flat) with Piano (1939). fp?

Organ Sonata No. 3, on old folksongs (1940). fp Tanglewood, Mass., 31 July 1940

Sonata for Cor Anglais and Piano (1941). fp New York, 23 November 1941

Sonata for Tenor Trombone and Piano (1941). fp?

Variations on an Old English Children's Song: 'A frog he went a-courting', for cello and piano (1941). fp?

'Little' Sonata (No. 2) for Cello and Piano (1942). fp?

Gay, for two cellos (c.1942). fp?

Four Pieces for Bassoon and Cello (1942). fp?

Six Easy Pieces for Bassoon and Cello (1943). fp?

Echo, for flute and piano (1942). fp?

Sonata for Alto Horn (in E flat) or Saxophone and Piano (1943). fp not known.

Ludus minor ('Small Game'), for cello and clarinet (1944). fp?

Sonata (No. 3) for Cello and Piano (1948). fp 1949

Sonata for Double Bass and Piano (1949). fp Vienna, 26 April 1950.

Sonata for Bass Tuba and Piano (1955). fp?

Arrangements

Serenade for Cello, by David Popper, arranged for piccolo, flute, two oboes, two bassoons, two horns and percussion (1919; lost). fp?

Cadenzas for violin and piano concertos by Mozart (1933; lost). fp?

Auslandische Lieder, ('Foreign Songs' from Switzerland, Iceland, China, Turkey, Serbia) arranged for clarinet and string quartet (1936; lost). fp?

Violin part for Concerto in D minor by Robert Schumann (ed., 1937). fp 1938

Orfeo, opera by Claudio Monteverdi (1943). fp?

Psalm 100, by Max Reger (1955). fp Cologne, 1955

Further Reading

This list contains the official sources of published material for *Hindemith, Hartmann and Henze* as well as items for further reading. I have restricted my selections for the latter mainly to book-length studies in English, available in book shops, music shops and libraries. The majority of the writing on all three composers is in German; to itemize all the many articles in this and other languages that have appeared in numerous journals going back across the century would be beyond the scope of this book. Those articles listed here are ones that yielded particular points taken into my narrative. The majority of the books listed below contain substantial bibliographies which can be used as guides for further reading. For ease of reference I have split the list into five categories: the first dealing with German political and economic history, the second with German music, followed by one for each composer.

German Political and Economic History

Given the major role of Germany in world affairs since the 1860s there are a good many studies on its history, from the earliest times onwards. One of the finest, which traces modern Germany from its roots over a millenium-and-a-half ago is Geoffrey Barraclough's *The Origins of Modern Germany*. A readable and informative general account covering the post-Napoleonic period to the present day is William Carr's *A History of Germany 1815–1990*, but for the Nazi period, William L. Shirer's *The Rise and Fall of the Third Reich*, is still the classic account. Of interest for their wider view taking in social and cultural matters are: *The Fontana History of Germany 1918–90: The Divided Nation* and *The Burden of German History 1919–45: Essays for the Goethe Institute*. For an account of the economic history pre-Weimar, *The German Empire 1871–1918* by Hans-Ulrich Wehler proved most helpful. A record made from the official British perspective of events in the Rhineland between the end of World War 1 and the evacuation of British troops in 1929 can be found in *The Occupation of the Rhineland 1918–29*, compiled for the Imperial War Museum. The extract from the tourist brochure, *The Muses on the Banks of the Spree*, was used as the epigraph to the poem *Apocalypse* by D. J. Enright, printed in *The New Poetry*, ed. A. Alvarez (Penguin, revised edition, 1966).

Barraclough, G. *The Origins of Modern Germany* (Oxford, Blackwell, 2nd edition, reprinted 1988)

Carr, W. *A History of Germany 1815–1990* (Sevenoaks, Edward Arnold, 4th edition, 1991)

Edmonds, J. E. *The Occupation of the Rhineland, 1918–29* (London, HMSO, 1987)

Fulbrook, M. *The Fontana History of Germany 1918–90: The Divided Nation* (London, Fontana Press, 1991)

Laffan, M. (ed.), *The Burden of German History 1919–45: Essays for the Goethe Institute* (London, Methuen, 1986)

Shirer, W. L. *The Rise and Fall of the Third Reich* (London, Secker and Warburg, 1960)

Wehler, H. U. *The German Empire 1871–1918*, translated by Kim Traynor (Leamington Spa and Dover, New Hampshire, Berg, 1985)

German Music

Beaumont, A. *Busoni the Composer* (London, Faber and Faber, 1985)

Boulez, P. *Orientations: Selected Writings*, J.J. Nattiez (ed.), translated by M. Cooper (London, Faber and Faber, 1992).

Drew, D. *Kurt Weill: A Handbook* (London, Faber and Faber, 1987)

Flesch, C. F. *'And do you also play the violin?'* (London, Toccata Press, 1990)

Furtwängler, W. *Furtwängler on Music: Essays and Addresses*, translated by R. Taylor (Aldershot, Scolar Press, 1991). Includes the famous article 'The Hindemith Case' and an open letter to Joseph Goebbels.

Heyworth, P. *Otto Klemperer: His Life and Times* (Cambridge, Cambridge University Press, 1983)

Klemperer, O. *Klemperer on Music: Shavings from a Musician's Workbench*, M. Anderson (ed.) (London, Toccata Press, 1986)

Kurtz, M. *Stockhausen: A Biography*, translated by R. Toop (London, Faber and Faber, 1992)

Leibowitz, R. *Schoenberg and his School: The Contemporary Stage of the Language of Music*, translated by Dika Newlin (Original French edition, Paris, 1947; translation New York, Da Capo, 1949)

Levi, E. *Music in the Third Reich* (London, Macmillan, 1994)

'Atonality, 12-tone music and the Third Reich', *Tempo* No. 178, September 1991

Lewinski, W.-E. von, 'The Variety of Trends in Modern German music' in P. H. Lang and N. Broder (eds.) *Contemporary Music in Europe: A Comprehensive Survey* (London, Dent, Schirmer, 1965)

Mäkelä, T. *Concertante Chamber Music in the Europe of the Early 1920s* (in Finnish, with English and German abstracts; Helsinki, 1990). From this was derived 'Concertante chamber music in the early 1920s', *Finnish Music Quarterly*, No. 1, 1990

Moldenhauer, H. with R. Moldenhauer *Anton von Webern: A Chronicle of his Life and Music* (London, Gollancz, 1978)

Stuckenschmidt, H. H. *Twentieth-Century Composers II: Germany and Central Europe* (London, Weidenfeld, 1970)

Of German Music (ed.) – Symposium (Oxford, Oswald Wolff, 1976). Of particular relevance are Eric Roseberry's essays 'Into the twentieth century' and 'Schoenberg and Hindemith: a parting of the ways?'

Walton, S. *William Walton – Behind the Façade* (London, Oxford University Press, 1988)

White, E. W. *Stravinsky: The Composer and his Works* (London, Faber and Faber, 1979)

Karl Amadeus Hartmann

Almost all of the published material on Hartmann is available in German only. The principal source book is the collection of essays and occasional writings by the composer himself, published as *Kleine schriften*, and which also contains essays about Hartmann by other writers, including Henze on the First Symphony. The only previous biography in English is by Dr Andrew D. McCredie, available as the introduction to his Thematic Catalogue. Another valuable source book is an anthology, *Karl Amadeus Hartmann und die Musica viva*. Further publications include the extended programme-book for a Hartmann festival *Bilder und Dokumente*. The official Schott catalogue contains short introductory essays in German and English by the pianist Siegfried Mauser and Henze, while several of the more recent publications of Hartmann's music, especially of newly prepared scores such as the *Sinfonia tragica* and *Klagegesang*, and the recording of three orchestral works by Koch-Schwann (see below), are prefaced by short introductory essays from Dr McCredie.

Hartmann, K. A. and others *Kleine Schriften* ('Lesser writings'), in German (Mainz, B. Schott's Söhne, 1965)

Hausler, J. 'Hartmann, Karl Amadeus', *Grove International Dictionary of Music and Musicians* (6th edition, London, 1986)

McCredie, A. D. *Karl Amadeus Hartmann – Sein Leben und Werk* ('His Life and Work'), in German (Wilhelmshaven, Heinrichshofen, 1980). An English version, available as the introduction to *Karl Amadeus Hartmann – Thematic Catalogue of his Works*, contains an exhaustive bibliography (Wilhelmshaven, Heinrichshofen, 1982)

Warnaby, J. 'Karl Amadeus Hartmann's *Klagegesang* and the Re-emergence of his Early Music', *Tempo* No. 180, March 1992

Various authors *Karl Amadeus Hartmann und die Musica Viva* (Schott/R. Piper and Co., 1980)

Bilder und Dokumente. Karl Amadeus Hartmann. Eine Ausstellung der Kölnmusik zum nordrhein-westfälischen Karl Amadeus Hartmann-Zyklus 1989, in German (Munich, 1989)

Hans Werner Henze

Despite his celebrity, there is very little biographical material available in print in English. Henze has been interviewed for many magazines but these concentrate usually on specific aspects – new works or a particular theme, e.g. politics (most are now out of date in any event). One of the most all-embracing was the television documentary by Tony Knox, *Orpheus Behind the Wire* (*The South Bank Show*, London Weekend Television, 1990). A large booklet in English was prepared for the BBC Henze festival at the Barbican (10–15 January 1991) which included an interview with Andrew Huth, essays by Henze, Ingeborg Bachmann and John Drummond plus a chronology, bibliography and discography all collated by Stephen Walsh. The main source book will eventually be Henze's autobiography, still incomplete at the time of going to press. In the meantime, his own collection of essays *Music and Politics: Collected Writings 1953–81* provides a wealth of biographical and musical information.

Geitel, K. *Hans Werner Henze*, in German (Berlin, Rembrandt, 1968)

Henderson, R. 'Henze, Hans Werner', *Grove International Dictionary of Music and Musicians* (6th edition, London, 1986)

Henze, H. W. *Music and Politics: Collected Writings 1953–81*, translated by Peter Labanyi (London, Faber and Faber, 1982)

Autobiography (in preparation)

Jacobsen, B. 'Henze, Hans Werner' in Brian Morton and Pamela Collins (eds.) *Contemporary Composers* (Chicago and London, St James Press, 1992)

Rexroth, D. (ed.) *Der Komponist Hans Werner Henze* ('The composer Hans Werner Henze') – symposium, in German (Mainz, Schott, 1986)

Various authors Programme book for the BBC Henze festival, 10–15 January 1991 (London)

Paul Hindemith

The definitive biography in English is Geoffrey Skelton's *Paul Hindemith – The Man Behind the Music*; in German it is Andras Briner's *Paul Hindemith* (Atlantis, 1971). Other books on the composer have tended to concern themselves more with purely musical issues, as with Ian Kemp's *Hindemith* and David Neumeyer's *The Music of Paul Hindemith*. The accompanying notes by Dr Giselher Schubert of the

Paul Hindemith Institute in Frankfurt am Main to Wergo's series of recordings (see Selective Discography below) are also highly informative in their own right. A photographic record of the composer is preserved in *Paul Hindemith – Zeugnis in Bildern* ('Testimony in Pictures') and *Paul Hindemith – Die letzten Jahre* ('The Final Years'), both published by B. Schott's Söhne. Several of Hindemith's students wrote about their teacher. *The Listener* featured three such items: 'The Music of Paul Hindemith' and 'Meditation' by Walter Leigh and an obituary by Franz Reizenstein, while Arnold Cooke penned a long article for *Music Survey* in 1949. Also of interest are *The Glenn Gould Reader*, presenting the Canadian pianist's penetrating if individual viewpoints, and Sir Donald Tovey's exposition on the *Kammermusik* No. 1 in *Essays in Musical Analysis*. For a very unsympathetic response to Hindemith, see Constant Lambert's *Music, Ho!*.

Aprahamian, F. (ed.) *Essays on music: An Anthology from* The Listener (London, Cassell, 1967)

Briner, A. *Paul Hindemith,* in German (Zürich, Atlantis, 1971)

Cooke, A. 'Paul Hindemith' in D. Mitchell and H. Keller (eds.) *Music Survey – New Series* (Volume II, Nos. 1 and 2, 1949; reprinted in anthology, London, Faber and Faber, 1981)

Gould, G. *The Glenn Gould Reader*, T. Page (ed.) (London, Faber and Faber, 1984)

Hindemith, P. *The Craft of Musical Composition*, Vol. I translated Arthur Mendel (London, Associated Music Publishers, 1937); Vol. II translated Otto Ortman (London, Associated Music Publishers, 1941); Volume III (Mainz, Schott, 1970)

Traditional Harmony (2nd edition, London, Associated Music Publishers, 1944)

Elementary Training for Musicians (revised edition, London, Schott, 1968)

[**Hindemith, P.**] *A Composer's World* (Harvard University Press, 1952)

Briefe ('Letters'), D. Rexroth (ed.) (Frankfurt, 1982)

Kemp, I. *Hindemith*, No. 6 in the 'Oxford Studies of Composers' (London, Oxford University Press, 1970)

Preface to the study score of the *Mathis der Maler* symphony (Eulenburg No. 573, 1984)

Lambert, C. *Music, Ho! A Study of Music in Decline* (3rd edition, London, Hogarth Press, 1948)

Leigh, W. 'The Music of Paul Hindemith', *The Listener*, 1935

'Meditation', *The Listener*, 1936

Neumeyer, D. *The music of Paul Hindemith*, in the series 'Composers of the Twentieth Century' (New Haven, Yale University Press, 1986)

Reizenstein, F. Obituary, *The Listener*, 1964

Skelton, G. *Paul Hindemith: The Man Behind the Music* (London, Gollancz, 1975)

Tovey, D. 'Chamber Music No. 1' in *Essays in Musical Analysis, Volume IV: Illustrative Music* (London, Oxford University Press, 1937)

Paul Hindemith – Zeugnis in Bildern 'Testimony in Pictures') (Mainz, Schott, 1955)

Paul Hindemith – Die letzten Jahre ('The Final Years') (Mainz, Schott, 1965)

Selective Discography

For ease of access, I have restricted my choice to CDs available at the time of writing.

Karl Amadeus Hartmann

Hartmann's discography is simple to compile since it is so meagre. By far the most important item is the pioneering Wergo four-CD set of the eight numbered symphonies plus *Gesangsszene*, performed with élan by the Bavarian Radio Symphony Orchestra under four different conductors: Fritz Rieger (No. 1), Ferdinand Leitner (No. 3), Rafael Kubelik (Nos. 2, 4–6, 8 plus *Gesangsszene*) and Zdenek Macal (No. 7). The first issues of two further cycles have been released by Karl Anton Rickenbacker (on Koch Schwann) and Ingo Metzmacher (EMI). The *Concerto funebre* has been recorded more often than any other Hartmann work (at least four times). The best is that by Thomas Zehetmair, who also directs the Deutsche Kammerphilharmonie; the reissued account by André Gertler has much to commend it, not least Paul Tortelier in Hindemith's 1940 Cello Concerto. Neither of the operas has been recorded.

Orchestral

Symphonies Nos. 1–8
Gesangsszene
Doris Soffel, Dietrich Fischer-Dieskau, Bavarian Radio Symphony Orchestra conducted by Fritz Rieger, Ferdinand Leitner, Rafael Kubelik, Zdenek Macal
WERGO WER 60187–50 (4 CDs)

Adagio: Symphony No. 2
Gesangsszene
Sinfonia tragica
Siegmund Nimsgern, Bamberg Symphony Orchestra conducted by Karl Anton Rickenbacker
KOCH SCHWANN 3–1295–2

Symphony No. 4, for String Orchestra
Bamberg Symphony Orchestra conducted by Ingo Metzmacher; with Messiaen's *Et exspecto resurrectionem mortuorum*
EMI CDC 7 54916 2

Concerto funebre, for Violin and Strings (revised version)
Thomas Zehetmair, Deutsche Kammerphilharmonie; with concertos by Berg and Janáček
TELDEC 2292–46449–2 (re-issued on 4509–97449–2)

Concerto funebre
André Gertler, Czech Philharmonic Orchestra conducted by Karel Ančerl; with Hindemith's Violin Concerto (1939), Cello Concerto (1940)
SUPRAPHON 11 1955–2 011

Concerto funebre
Hans Maile, Berlin Radio Symphony Orchestra conducted by Alexander Sander; with concertos by Bernd Alois Zimmermann and Werner Egk
KOCH SCHWANN 3–1075–2 H1

Lied for Trumpet and Wind Instruments (surviving movement of Trumpet Concerto, 1932–3)
Juoko Harjame, Finnish Radio Symphony Orchestra conducted by Jukka-Pekka Saraste; with concertos by Haydn, Hummel, Gruner and Zimmerman
FINLANDIA 4509–96868–2

Chamber/Instrumental

String Quartet No. 1: 'Carillon'
String Quartet No. 2
Pellegrini Quartet
CPO 999 219–2

Piano Sonata No. 2: '27 April 1945'
Jazz Toccata and Fugue
Sonatina
Little Suites Nos. 1 and 2
Siegried Mauser (piano)
VIRGIN CLASSICS VC 7 91170–2

Hans Werner Henze

There are several large gaps in Henze's representation on CD, not least due to Deutsche Grammophon's failure to issue much of its back catalogue. This will presumably be rectified in the run-up to Henze's seventieth birthday in July 1996. The limited-edition eight-disc collection listed below contains many works in the backlog, which have begun to appear separately at the time of going to press (most notably *Der junge Lord*). Henze as interpreter of his own music is represented solely by a two-CD set of his first six symphonies, in performances that are unlikely to be surpassed in authority. Of equal stature, though, is Simon Rattle's blistering live account with the City of Birmingham Symphony Orchestra of No. 7 for EMI, coupled with the *Barcarola.* Rattle is likely to record its successor, and the fashion for live recordings has also yielded Metzmacher's account of the small orchestral *Requiem*, actually a composite of several concert performances. A disc worthy of note in connection with Henze is that devoted to music by his friend and erstwhile mentor, Paul Dessau, featuring the orchestral *Bach Variations*, Piano Sonatina, Sonatina for small orchestra and piano obbligato, Sixth String Quartet and *Music for 15 Strings* (Pilz 44 2077–2).

Collections

Elegy for Young Lovers (excerpts)
Der langwierige Weg in die Wohnung der Natascha Ungeheuer
Der junge Lord
The Raft of the 'Medusa'
El Cimarrón (original version)
Cantata della fiaba estrema
Whispers from Heavenly Death
Being Beauteous
Essay on Pigs
Sicilian Muses
Moralities
Various soloists, orchestras and conductors
Deutsche Grammophon 437 653/660–2 (8 CDs)

Opera

Boulevard Solitude
Various soloists, Orchestre de Rencontres conducted by Ivan Anguelov
Cascavelle VEL 1006 (2 CDs)

Der junge Lord
Edith Mathis, Donald Grobe, soloists, Deutsche Oper Chorus and Orchestra conducted by Christoph von Dohnanyi
Deutsche Grammophon 445 248–2GC2
(2 CDs from 437 653/660–2 above)

The Bassarids (excluding 'The Judgment of Calliope')
Various soloists, RIAS Chamber Choir, Berlin Radio Symphony Orchestra conducted by Gerd Albrecht
Koch Schwann 314 006K3 (2 CDs)

La Cubana (original version)
Various soloists including Anja Silja, Hamburg Radio Choir and Chamber Orchestra conducted by Jan Latham-König
Wergo WER 60129/30–2 (2 CDs)

The English Cat
Various soloists, Parnassus Orchestra (London), conducted by Markus Stenz
Wergo WER 6204–2 (2 CDs)

Orchestral

Symphonies Nos. 1–6
Berlin Philharmonic Orchestra, London Symphony Orchestra conducted by Hans Werner Henze
Deutsche Grammophon 429 854–2 (2 CDs)

Ragtimes and Habaneras (arranged David Purser)
London Brass conducted by David Purser; with works by various other composers
Teldec 243 713–2

Requiem (Nine Sacred Concertos)
Ueli Wiget, Håkan Hardenberger, Ensemble Modern conducted by Ingo Metzmacher
Sony Classical SK 58972

Symphony No. 7
Barcarola
City of Birmingham Symphony Orchestra conducted by Simon Rattle
EMI Classics 7 54762 2

Le Miracle de la Rose: Imaginary Theatre II
An eine Äolsharfe
Hans Deinzer, David Tanenbaum, Ensemble Modern conducted by Hans Werner Henze
Ars Musici AM 0859–2

Vocal/Choral

Kammermusik 1958
Neill Jenkins, Timothy Walker, Scharoun Ensemble conducted by Brynmor Llewellyn-Jones
Koch CD 310 004 H1

El Cimarrón (revised version)
Paul Yoder, Michael Faust, Reinbert Evers, Mircea Ardeleanu
Koch CD 314 030 K2 (2 CDs)

Voices (complete)
Roswitha Trexler, Joachim Vogt; members of Leipzig Radio Symphony Orchestra conducted by Horst Neumann
Berlin Classics 0021802 BC (2 CDs)

Voices (extract of seventeen songs)
Gudrun Pelker, Frieder Lang, Musik Fabrik NRW conducted by Johann Kalitzke
CPO 999 192–2

Orpheus behind the Wire
Danish National Radio Chamber Choir conducted by Stefan Parkman; with works by Lidholm, Schoenberg, Nørgård and Poulenc
Chandos CHAN 8963

Chamber/Instrumental

String Quartets Nos. 1–5
Arditti Quartet
Wergo WER 60114/5 –50 (2 CDs)

Royal Winter Music: Two Sonatas on Shakespearean Characters
Dietmar Kres (guitar)
Wergo 60126–50

Une petite phrase
Variations for Piano, Op. 13
Lucy Escott Variations
Divertimenti for Two Pianos
Sechs Stücke für junge Pianisten
Cherubino, three miniatures (1980–1)
Piano Sonata
Homero Francesch (piano)
Wergo WER 6239–2

Paul Hindemith

Hindemith's music – or at least a substantial part of it – has been relatively well served on disc from the 1930s onwards. The vast majority of these recordings, issued on vinyl, have long been unavailable. His centenary in 1995 will no doubt bring many of these back into public view as well as provoke new recordings. The two largest operas, *Mathis der Maler* and *Die Harmonie der Welt*, exemplify these categories. EMI's 1979 recording of *Mathis*, conducted by Rafael Kubelík with Fischer-Dieskau in the title role, was only released on CD in Hindemith's centenary year (in the meantime, Wergo issued a new one). Decca have announced that they will record *Die Harmonie der Welt* as part of their *Entartete Musik* series (a trifle bizarrely since the work was composed eleven years after the fall of the Nazis) for release to coincide with the centenary in November 1995. The entire ballet *Nobilissima Visione* has been recorded by conductor Karl Anton Rickenbacker for Koch-Schwann (1994, yet to be issued). Of the recordings that are available, the ideal introduction to Hindemith's mature style can be found on Herbert

Blomstedt's immaculate disc for Decca of the *Mathis der Maler* Symphony, *Trauermusik* and *Symphonic Metamorphoses.* (An enterprising alternative for the third of those works occurs on a Chandos disc by Neeme Järvi, pairing Hindemith's reworkings with the Weber originals.) One of the most acclaimed recordings of recent times is that by Riccardo Chailly and the Amsterdam Concertgebouw of the seven *Kammermusik* and *Kleine Kammermusik* (Decca, 1992).

Few of Hindemith's own recordings have survived in the catalogue (Deutsche Grammophon-Gesellschaft deleted several in the early 1990s), but EMI's compilation of the *Nobilissima Visione* suite, Horn Concerto (with Dennis Brain), the *Konzertmusik* (Op. 50) and Symphony in B flat is revelatory (EMI, 1990; recorded in 1958–9 and re-issued in 1994 with the Clarinet Concerto and some chamber pieces). So is another of recordings from between 1926 and 1934, featuring the composer as conductor – in the *Mathis der Maler* Symphony with the Berlin Philharmonic just a month after the première – and as violist, in the Second String Trio – with Goldberg and Feuermann – and the Third String Quartet with the Amar Quartet (including his brother Rudolf on the cello).

Collections

Nobilissima Visione: Suite
Horn Concerto
Clarinet Concerto
Konzertmusik, Op. 50
Symphony in B flat
Viola Sonata
Scherzo for Viola and Cello
Various soloists, Philharmonia Orchestra conducted by Paul Hindemith (rec. 1934–59)
EMI CDS5 55032–2

Symphony: Mathis der Maler
String Trio No. 2
String Quartet No. 3, Op. 22
Berlin Philharmonic Orchestra conducted by Paul Hindemith; Goldberg–Hindemith–Feuermann Trio; Amar Quartet (rec. 1926–34)
Koch Schwann 3–1134–2

Der Schwanendreher – Viola Concerto
Trauermusik
Sonata for Piano, four hands
Sonata for Viola and Piano No. 3
Paul Hindemith (viola, piano), Jesus Maria Sanromá (piano), Arthur Fiedler's Sinfonietta, string orchestra conducted by Bruno Reibold
Biddulph LAB 087

Opera and Ballet

Mörder, Hoffnung der Frauen
Der Dämon
Various soloists, RIAS Chamber Choir, Berlin Radio Symphony Orchestra conducted by Gerd Albrecht
Wergo WER 60132–50

Das Nusch-Nuschi
Various soloists, Berlin Radio Symphony Orchestra conducted by Gerd Albrecht
Wergo WER 60146–50

Sancta Susanna
Three Songs, Op. 9
Helen Donath, Gabriele Schnaut, Gabriele Schreckenbach, Janis Martin, RIAS Chamber Choir, Berlin Radio Symphony Orchestra conducted by Gerd Albrecht
Wergo WER 60106–50

Der Dämon
Hérodiade
Siegfried Mauser, Frankfurt Radio Symphony Orchestra conducted by Werner Andreas Albert
CPO 999 220-2

Cardillac (original version)
Mathis der Maler (excerpts)
Dietrich Fischer-Dieskau, Leonore Kirschstein, Donald Grobe, Eberhard Katz, Elisabeth Söderström, Cologne Radio Choir and Symphony Orchestra conducted by Joseph Keilberth
Deutsche Grammophon 431 741–2 (2 CDs)

Neues vom Tage (original version)
Various soloists, Cologne State Music School Choir, Cologne Radio Symphony Orchestra conducted by Jan Latham-König
Wergo WER 6192–2

Mathis der Maler
James King, Dietrich Fischer-Dieskau, William Cochran, other soloists, Bavarian Radio Choir and Symphony Orchestra conducted by Rafael Kubelík
EMI CD55 55237–2 (3 CDs)

Mathis der Maler
Josef Protschka, Roland Herrmann, Harald Stamm, other soloists, Cologne Radio Choir and Symphony Orchestra conducted by Gerd Albrecht
Wergo WER 6255–2

Orchestral

Kammermusik Nos. 1–7
Kleine Kammermusik, Op. 24 No. 2
Various soloists, Royal Concertgebouw Orchestra, Amsterdam, conducted by Riccardo Chailly
Decca 433 816–2 (2 CDs)

Kammermusik No. 4, Op. 36 No. 3
David Oistrakh, Moscow Radio Symphony Orchestra conducted by Genadi Rozhdestvensky; with works by Bartók and Syzmanowski
Forlane UCD 16589

Symphony: Mathis der Maler
Trauermusik
Symphonic Metamorphoses on Themes by Carl Maria von Weber
San Francisco Symphony Orchestra conducted by Herbert Blomstedt
Decca 421 523–2

Violin Concerto (1939)
Cello Concerto (1940)
André Gertler, Paul Tortelier, Czech Philharmonic Orchestra conducted by Karel Ančerl; with Hartmann's *Concerto funebre*
Supraphon 11 1955–2 011

Kammermusik No. 5, Op. 36 No. 4
Trauermusik
Der Schwanendreher – Viola Concerto (1935)
Georg Schmid, Bavarian Radio Symphony Orchestra conducted by Rafael Kubelík
Koch Schwann CD 11734

Symphony: Mathis der Maler
Violin Concerto (1939)
Symphonic Metamorphoses on Themes by Carl Maria von Weber
Suisse Romande Orchestra conducted by Paul Kletzki; David Oistrakh, London Symphony Orchestra conducted by Paul Hindemith (rec. 1962); London Symphony Orchestra conducted by Claudio Abbado
Decca 433 081–2

Symphony: Mathis der Maler
Noblissima Visione
Symphonic Metamorphoses on Themes by Carl Maria von Weber
The Philadelphia Orchestra conducted by Wolfgang Sawallisch
EMI Classics CDC 5 55230 2

Cello Concerto (1940)
The Four Temperaments
Rafael Wallfisch, BBC Philharmonic Orchestra conducted by Yan Pascal Tortelier
Chandos CHAN 9124

Symphony in E flat
Nobilissima Visione: Suite
Neues vom Tage: Overture
BBC Philharmonic Orchestra conducted by Yan Pascal Tortelier
Chandos CHAN 9060

Symphonia Serena
Die Harmonie der Welt: Symphony
BBC Philharmonic Orchestra conducted by Yan Pascal Tortelier
Chandos CHAN 9217

Organ Concerto
Kammermusik No. 7, Op. 46 No. 2, Organ Concerto
Suite for a Mechanical Organ (Das triadische Ballet)
Martin Haselböck, Wiener Symphoniker conducted by Rafael Frühbeck de Burgos
Koch Schwann 3–1202–2H1

Vocal/Choral

Die junge Magd
Des Todes Tod
Gabriele Schnaut, Gabriele Schreckenbach, members of the Berlin Radio Symphony Orchestra conducted by Gerd Albrecht
Wergo WER 60117–50

Das Marienleben (revised version)
Anneliese Kupper (soprano), Carl Seemann (piano)
Christophorus CD 74612

Orchestral Songs from Das Marienleben (revised version)
Karita Mattila, Lahti Symphony Orchestra conducted by Ulf Söderblom; with works by Sallinen and Aarre Merikanto
Finlandia FACD 359

Selected Songs
Dietrich Fischer-Dieskau (baritone), Aribert Reimann (piano)
Orfeo C 156 861 A

When Lilacs Last in the Door-yard Bloom'd
Various soloists, Atlanta Symphony Orchestra and Choir conducted by Robert Shaw
Telarc CD 80132

When Lilacs Last in the Door-yard Bloom'd
Various soloists, Schola Cantorum, New York Philharmonic Orchestra conducted by Paul Hindemith
CBS CD 45881

Mass
Twelve Madrigals
Six Chansons
Netherlands Chamber Choir conducted by Uwe Gronostay
Globe GLO 5125

Chamber/Instrumental

Morgenmusik
Trumpet Sonata
Trombone Sonata
Tuba Sonata
Recorder Trio
Alto Saxophone Sonata
Bassoon Sonata
Various soloists
BIS–CD–159

String Quartet in F minor, Op. 2
String Quartet No. 4, Op. 32
Sonare Quartet
CPO 999 001–2

String Quartet No. 3, Op. 22
Brandis Quartet; with works by Schulhoff and Weill
Nimbus NI 5410

Dance of the Wooden Dolls (from 'Tuttifäntchen')
Suite: '1922', Op. 26
Five Dance Pieces, Op. 19
Klaviermusik, Op. 37, Part 1
Georg Friedrich Schenck (piano)
Koch Schwann CD 310 007 H1

In einer Nacht, Op. 15
Piano Sonata, Op. 17 (recon. B. Billeter)
Lied
Berceuse
Klavierstück für Frau Josefine Grosz
Variations (1936)
Two Fugues from 'Ludus tonalis'
Bernhard Billeter (piano)
Jecklin-Disco JD 644–2

Five Dance Pieces, Op. 18
In einer Nacht, Op. 15
Suite: '1922', Op. 26
Lied
Kleines Klavierstück
Berceuse
Hans Petermandl (piano)
Marco Polo 8.223335

Klaviermusik, Op. 37
Piano Sonata, Op. 17 (recon. B. Billeter)
Two Little Pieces (1934)
Hans Petermandl (piano)
Marco Polo 8.223336

Piano Sonatas Nos. 1–3
Glenn Gould (piano)
CBS MPK 45689 (deleted; re-issued as part of a Sony multi-volume set devoted to Gould)

Piano Sonatas Nos. 1–3
Variations (1936)
Hans Petermandl (piano)
Marco Polo 8.223337

Organ Sonatas Nos. 1–3
Piet Kee (organ); with works by Reger
Chandos CHAN 9097

Ludus tonalis
Kleine Klaviermusik
Hans Petermandl (piano)
Marco Polo 8.223338

Ludus tonalis
Piano Sonata No. 2
Sviatoslav Richter (piano)
Pyramid 13497

Ludus tonalis
Suite '1922', Op. 26
John McCabe (piano)
Hyperion (in preparation)

Sonatas for Solo Viola Nos. 1–4
Nobuko Imai (viola)
BIS–CD–571

Sonatas for Viola and Piano Nos. 1–3
Meditation, from 'Nobilissima Visione'
Nobuko Imai (viola), Roland Pöntinen (piano)
BIS–CD–651

Septet for Wind Instruments
Deutsche Kammerphilharmonie; with works by Toch and Weill
Virgin Classics VC 45056–2

Index

Page numbers in italics refer to picture captions.

Photographic Acknowledgements

The publishers would like to thank Almuth Willing at Schott, and Luitgard Schader and Dr Giselher Schubert of the Paul-Hindemith-Institut for their help with photographic material.

AEG, Frankfurt: 24–5
Archiv für Kunst und Geschichte, London: 28, 29, 35, 36–7, 38t+b, 52t+b, 66, 71, 75, 76–7, 100, 102–3, 111, 129t+b, 146t
Bayerische Staatsbibliothek, Munich: 93, 105, 152, 153l+r
The British Architectural Library, RIBA, London: 56
Deutsche Luftbild, Hamburg: 142–3
Hulton-Deutsch Collection, London: 18, 20, 21, 32, 34, 41, 45, 47, 62–3, 69, 73, 78, 79, 97, 112–3, 114, 115, 119, 121, 122–3, 139, 140, 146b, 151, 156, 157, 158–9, 163, 164, 173, 177, 188–9 (photo © Steve Eason)